Busy Ant Maths

Stretch and Challenge 1

A problem-solving, cross-curricular programme for children working above end-of-year expectations

Peter Clarke

William Collins' dream of knowledge for all began with the publication of his first book in 1819. A self-educated mill worker, he not only enriched millions of lives, but also founded a flourishing publishing house. Today, staying true to this spirit, Collins books are packed with inspiration, innovation and practical expertise. They place you at the centre of a world of possibility and give you exactly what you need to explore it.

Collins. Freedom to teach.

Published by Collins

An imprint of HarperCollinsPublishers
The News Building
1 London Bridge Street
London SE1 9GF

Browse the complete Collins catalogue at
www.collins.co.uk

10 9 8 7 6 5 4 3 2 1

ISBN 978-0-00-816730-1

British Library Cataloguing in Publication Data
A Catalogue record for this publication is available from the British Library.

Commissioned by Fiona McGlade
Cover and series design by Kneath Associates
Template creation by Ken Vail Graphic Design
Illustrations by Mark Walker, Steve Evans, Gwyneth Williamson and QBS Learning
Typesetting by QBS Learning
Editing and proofreading by Alissa McWhinnie

Printed and bound by Printed by CPI Group (UK) Ltd, Croydon, CR0 4YY

Acknowledgements
Peter Clarke wishes to thank Brian Molyneaux for his valuable contribution to this publication.

Contents

Domain(s)	Topic	Issue number	Teacher's notes page number
Number: – Number and place value	Number	1	94
	Number	2	97
	Number	3	100
	Number	4	103
Number: – Addition and subtraction	Addition	5	106
	Addition	6	109
	Subtraction	7	112
	Subtraction	8	115
Number: – Multiplication and division	Multiplication	9	118
	Multiplication	10	121
	Division	11	124
	Division	12	127
Number: – Addition and subtraction – Multiplication and division	Mixed operations	13	130
	Mixed operations	14	134
	Mixed operations	15	137
	Mixed operations	16	140
	Mixed operations	17	143
	Mixed operations	18	146
Number: – Fractions	Fractions	19	149
	Fractions	20	152
	Fractions	21	155
Measurement	Length and height	22	158
	Weight and mass	23	161
	Capacity and volume	24	164
	Time	25	167
	Measurement	26	170
	Measurement	27	173
Geometry: – Properties of shapes	2-D shapes	28	176
	3-D shapes	29	179
	Patterns	30	182
Geometry: – Position and direction	Position and direction	31	185
	Movement	32	188
Geometry: – Properties of shapes – Position and direction	Geometry	33	191
	Geometry	34	194
Statistics *	Statistics	35	197
	Statistics	36	200

* Although statistics is not in the Year 1 Mathematics Programme of Study, two Issues have been included in *Stretch and Challenge 1* in order to develop skills such as sorting, classifying and comparing data. These Issues also aim to provide further opportunities for children to meet the following aims of the National Curriculum for Mathematics:

– *reason mathematically by following a line of enquiry, conjecturing relationships and generalisations, and developing an argument, justification or proof using mathematical language*

– *... solve problems by applying their mathematics to a variety of routine and non-routine problems with increasing sophistication, including breaking down problems into a series of simpler steps and persevering in seeking solutions.*

Introduction

The National Curriculum emphasises the importance of all children mastering the programme of study taught each year and discourages the acceleration of children into content from subsequent years.

The National Curriculum states: *'The expectation is that the majority of pupils will move through the programmes of study at broadly the same pace. However, decisions about when to progress should always be based on the security of pupils' understanding and their readiness to progress to the next stage. Pupils who grasp concepts rapidly should be challenged through being offered rich and sophisticated problems before any acceleration through new content. Those who are not sufficiently fluent with earlier material should consolidate their understanding, including through additional practice, before moving on.'* [1]

However, the National Curriculum also goes on to say that: *'Within each key stage, schools [therefore] have the flexibility to introduce content earlier or later than set out in the programme of study. In addition, schools can introduce key stage content during an earlier key stage, if appropriate.'* [2]

Stretch and Challenge aims to provide support in meeting the needs of those children who are exceeding age-related expectations by providing a range of problem-solving and cross-curricular activities designed to enrich and deepen children's mathematical knowledge, skills and understanding.

The series provides opportunities for children to reason mathematically and to solve increasingly complex problems, doing so with fluency, as described in the aims of the National Curriculum:

'The National Curriculum for mathematics aims to ensure that all pupils:

- *become* **fluent** *in the fundamentals of mathematics, including through varied and frequent practice with increasingly complex problems over time, so that pupils develop conceptual understanding and the ability to recall and apply knowledge rapidly and accurately*

- **reason mathematically** *by following a line of enquiry, conjecturing relationships and generalisations, and developing an argument, justification or proof using mathematical language*

- *can* **solve problems** *by applying their mathematics to a variety of routine and non-routine problems with increasing sophistication, including breaking down problems into a series of simpler steps and persevering in seeking solutions.'* [3]

Stretch and Challenge has been designed to provide:

- a flexible 'dip-in' resource that can easily be adapted to meet the needs of individual children, and different classroom and school organisational arrangements

- enrichment activities that require children to use and apply their mathematical knowledge, skills and understanding to reason mathematically and to solve increasingly complex problems

- mathematical activities linked to the entire primary curriculum, thereby ensuring a range of cross-curricular contexts

- an easy-to-use bank of activities to save teachers time in thinking up new enrichment activities

- an interesting, unique and consistent approach to presenting enrichment activities to children.

The *Stretch and Challenge* series consists of six packs, also available digitally on Collins Connect, one for each year group from Year 1 to Year 6.

---

1 Mathematics programmes of study: key stages 1 and 2 National Curriculum in England, September 2013, page 3

2 Mathematics programmes of study: key stages 1 and 2 National Curriculum in England, September 2013, page 4

3 Mathematics programmes of study: key stages 1 and 2 National Curriculum in England, September 2013, page 3

Printed resources

Containing:

- Pupil activity booklets (Issues)
- Teacher's notes
- Resource sheets

Online resources at connect.collins.co.uk

Containing editable:

- Pupil activity booklets (Issues)
- Teacher's notes
- Resource sheets

It is envisaged that the activities in *Stretch and Challenge* will be used by either individuals or pairs of children. However, given the flexible nature of the resource, if appropriate, children can work in groups. The activities are intended to be used:

- as additional work to be done once children have finished other set work

- by those children who grasp concepts rapidly and need to be challenged through rich and sophisticated problems

- as in-depth work that is to be undertaken over a prolonged period of time, such as during the course of several lessons, a week or a particular unit of work

- as a resource for promoting mathematical reasoning and problem solving and developing independent thinking and learning

- as a springboard for further investigations into mathematics based on the children's suggestions.

The features of *Stretch and Challenge*

Pupil activity booklets (Issues)

- Each of the 36 Issues in *Stretch and Challenge 1* consists of a four-page A5 pupil activity booklet (to be printed double sided onto one sheet of A4 paper).

- The 36 Issues cover the different domains and attainment targets of the Mathematics National Curriculum Programme of Study (see pages 11–16).

- The Issues have been designed to resemble a newspaper, with each of the Issues consisting of between five and eight different activities, all related to the same mathematical topic.

- It is important to note that children are not expected to complete all the activities in an Issue nor work their way through an Issue from beginning to end. For many children not all of the activities offered in an Issue will be appropriate. When choosing which activities a child is to complete, teachers should ensure that the activities do not accelerate the child into mathematical content they may not be familiar with, or are unable to reason more deeply in order to develop a conceptual understanding. Rather, activities should be chosen on the basis that they engage the child in reasoning and the development of mathematical thinking, as well as enriching and deepening the child's mathematical knowledge, skills and understanding.

- The terms 'Issue' and 'Volume' have been used rather than 'Unit' and 'Year group' because they are in keeping with the newspaper theme.

Types of activities

- Each of the 36 Issues in *Stretch and Challenge 1* are designed to deepen children's mathematical knowledge, skills and understandings, and enhance their use and application of mathematics. There are four different types of 'using and applying' activities in the series:

 What's the Problem?   The Puzzler

 Looking for Patterns   Let's Investigate

- Alongside developing children's problem-solving skills, the series also provides activities with cross-curricular links to other subjects in the primary curriculum. The following shows the *Stretch and Challenge* features and its corresponding primary curriculum subject.

Curriculum subject		*Stretch and Challenge* feature
English		The Language of Maths
Science		Focus on Science
Computing		Technology Today
Geography		Around the World
History		In the Past
Art and design / Music		The Arts Roundup
Design and Technology		Construct
Physical Education		Sports Update

- As well as the features mentioned above, other regular features in *Stretch and Challenge* include:

 Money Matters   At Home (home–school link activities).

- A chart showing the link between the Issues, the *Stretch and Challenge* features and cross-curricular links can be found on pages 17 and 18.

- Inquisitive ant is a recurring feature of the series. In each Issue there is an ant holding a mathematical word or symbol. Children locate the ant and write about the meaning of the word or symbol.

Teacher's notes

Each of the 36 Issues includes a set of teacher's notes, including answers.

Issue number

Prerequisites for learning

Lists the prerequisites for learning that children need to have acquired prior to this Issue.

Lists the associated knowledge and skills that contribute to understanding the Issue topic.

Simplifications ⬇

Where appropriate, offers suggestions for supporting children who may be experiencing difficulties understanding the main mathematical ideas.

Extensions ⬆

Where appropriate, offers suggestions for extending children's understanding if you feel they are developing a good understanding of the main mathematical ideas.

Assessment for Learning

Each Issue includes a list of questions specifically designed to assist in assessing pupils' understanding of the Issue topic.

Answers

These are provided where appropriate.

Mathematics topic

Resources

To aid preparation, the resources needed for the Issue are listed.

Teaching support

Provides teaching points for each of the activities in the Issue. These may be helpful when introducing the Issue to the children, or when children experience difficulty whilst working on a particular activity.

Almost all of the activities in *Stretch and Challenge* can be undertaken either individually or in pairs (or sometimes in small groups).

Where an activity is particularly suitable for pairs to work on, this is denoted by 👤 👤.

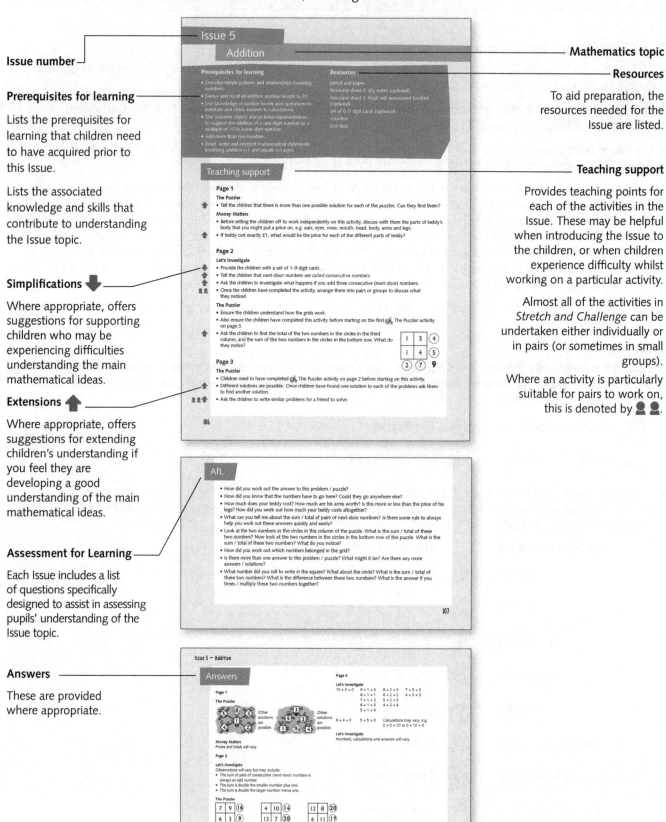

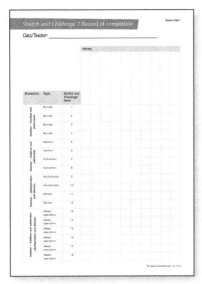

Record of completion

To assist in keeping a record of which Issues children have completed.

Once a child has completed an Issue you could either put a tick or write the date in the corresponding box.

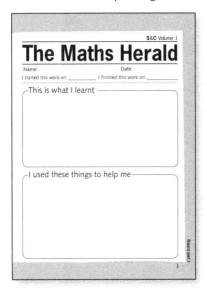

Pupil self assessment booklet

Each Resource Pack in the *Stretch and Challenge* series includes an age-appropriate pupil self assessment A5 booklet (to be printed double sided onto one sheet of A4 paper).

This booklet is a generic sheet that can be used for any, or all, of the 36 Issues in the Resource Pack.

The booklet is designed to provide children with an opportunity to undertake some form of self assessment once they have completed the Issue.

After the children have completed the booklet, discuss with them what they have written.

This can then be kept, together with the child's copy of the Issue and their working out and answers, including, if appropriate, 'My notes'.

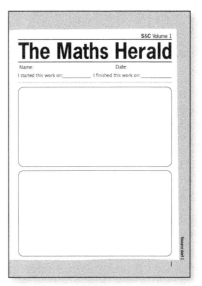

My notes

The pupil activity booklets have been designed to resemble a newspaper. This means that quite often there is insufficient space in the booklets for children to show their working and answers.

You may decide to simply provide children with pencil and paper to record their work or an exercise book that they use as their *'Stretch and Challenge* Journal'. Alternatively, you could provide them with a copy of the A5 booklet: 'My notes' (to be printed doubled sided onto one sheet of A4 paper). This can then be kept, together with the child's copy of the Issue and, if appropriate, their 'Pupil self assessment booklet.'

Whichever method you choose for the children to record their working and answers, i.e. on sheets of paper, using a 'My notes' booklet, in an exercise book, or any other method, children need to be clear and systematic in their recording.

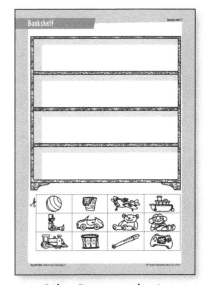

Other Resource sheets

For some of the activities, children are required to use a specific Resource sheet.

These are included both in the back of this Resource Pack and on the CD-ROM.

A possible *Stretch and Challenge* teaching and learning sequence

As the diagram on the right illustrates, the process of learning about mathematics can be thought of as the interrelationship between knowledge, understanding and application.

A suggested teaching sequence for working with children based on this model and using the activities in *Stretch and Challenge* is given below.

A complete sequence may occur during a particular lesson if the activity given is designed to be completed during the course of the lesson. Alternatively, the teaching and learning sequence may extend for a longer period of time if the activities are to be completed over the course of several lessons, a week or during a particular unit of work.

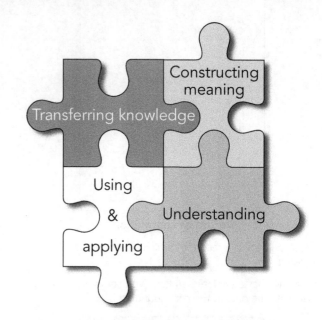

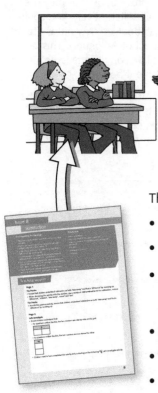

Briefing

The teacher:

- introduces the topic

- checks prerequisites for learning

- introduces the activity including, where appropriate, reading through the activity with the children

- checks for understanding

- clarifies any misconceptions

- ensures there is easy access to any necessary resources.

Working

- Children work individually, in pairs, or if appropriate, in groups.

- Teacher acts only as a 'guide-on-the-side'.

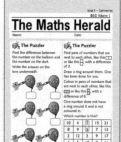

De-briefing

The child / children:

- reports back to others

- reflects on their learning

- identifies the 'next step'.

The teacher evaluates learning.

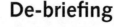

Links to the Year 1 Mathematics National Curriculum Programme of Study and Attainment Targets

Stretch and Challenge Issue

	1	2	3	4	5	6	7	8	9	10	11	12	13	14	15	16	17	18	19	20	21	22	23	24	25	26	27	28	29	30	31	32	33	34	35	36
Number – Number and place value																																				
• count to and across 100, forwards and backwards, beginning with 0 or 1, or from any given number	•	•	•	•		•	•	•	•	•	•																							•		•
• count, read and write numbers to 100 in numerals; count in multiples of twos, fives and tens	•	•	•			•	•	•	•	•	•	•	•	•	•	•	•																	•		•
• given a number, identify one more and one less	•	•	•																																	
• identify and represent numbers using objects and pictorial representations including the number line, and use the language of: equal to, more than, less than (fewer), most, least	•	•	•	•		•	•	•	•	•	•	•	•	•	•																			•		•
• read and write numbers from 1 to 20 in numerals and words	•	•	•	•		•	•	•	•	•	•	•	•	•	•	•	•	•	•	•																•
Notes and guidance (non-statutory)																																				
Pupils practice counting (1, 2, 3…), ordering (for example, first, second, third…), and to indicate a quantity (for example, 3 apples, 2 centimetres), including solving simple concrete problems, until they are fluent.	•	•	•	•		•	•	•	•	•	•	•	•	•	•	•														•						
Pupils begin to recognise place value in numbers beyond 20 by reading, writing, counting and comparing numbers up to 100, supported by objects and pictorial representations.	•	•	•	•		•	•	•	•	•	•	•	•	•	•	•	•													•						•
They practise counting as reciting numbers and counting as enumerating objects, and counting in twos, fives and tens from different multiples to develop their recognition of patterns in the number system (for example, odd and even numbers), including varied and frequent practice through increasingly complex questions.	•	•	•	•		•	•	•	•	•	•	•	•	•	•	•	•	•	•	•	•													•		•
They recognise and create repeating patterns with objects and with shapes.	•	•	•			•	•	•	•	•	•																•	•	•		•	•	•			

Stretch and Challenge Issue

Number – Addition and subtraction

	1	2	3	4	5	6	7	8	9	10	11	12	13	14	15	16	17	18	19	20	21	22	23	24	25	26	27	28	29	30	31	32	33	34	35	36
• read, write and interpret mathematical statements involving addition (+), subtraction (–) and equals (=) signs					•	•	•	•					•	•	•	•	•	•																		
• represent and use number bonds and related subtraction facts within 20					•	•	•	•					•	•	•	•	•	•																		
• add and subtract one-digit and two-digit numbers to 20, including zero					•	•	•	•						•	•	•	•	•																		
• solve one-step problems that involve addition and subtraction, using concrete objects and pictorial representations, and missing number problems such as 7 = ☐ – 9					•								•	•	•	•	•	•																		

Notes and guidance (non-statutory)

	1	2	3	4	5	6	7	8	9	10	11	12	13	14	15	16	17	18	19	20	21	22	23	24	25	26	27	28	29	30	31	32	33	34	35	36
Pupils memorise and reason with number bonds to 10 and 20 in several forms (for example, 9 + 7 = 16; 16 – 7 = 9; 7 = 16 – 9). They should realise the effect of adding or subtracting zero. This establishes addition and subtraction as related operations.													•		•			•																		
Pupils combine and increase numbers, counting forwards and backwards.					•	•	•	•					•	•	•			•																		
They discuss and solve problems in familiar practical contexts, including using quantities. Problems should include the terms: put together, add, altogether, total, take away, distance between, difference between, more than and less than, so that pupils develop the concept of addition and subtraction and are enabled to use these operations flexibly.					•		•	•					•	•	•			•																		

12

Stretch and Challenge Issue

Number – Multiplication and division

	1	2	3	4	5	6	7	8	9	10	11	12	13	14	15	16	17	18	19	20	21	22	23	24	25	26	27	28	29	30	31	32	33	34	35	36
solve one-step problems involving multiplication and division, by calculating the answer using concrete objects, pictorial representations and arrays with the support of the teacher									•	•	•	•	•	•	•	•	•																			

Notes and guidance (non-statutory)

	1	2	3	4	5	6	7	8	9	10	11	12	13	14	15	16	17	18	19	20	21	22	23	24	25	26	27	28	29	30	31	32	33	34	35	36
Through grouping and sharing small quantities, pupils begin to understand: multiplication and division; doubling numbers and quantities; and finding simple fractions of objects, numbers and quantities.									•	•	•	•	•	•	•	•	•																			
They make connections between arrays, number patterns, and counting in twos, fives and tens.									•	•	•	•	•	•	•	•	•																			

Number – Fractions

	1	2	3	4	5	6	7	8	9	10	11	12	13	14	15	16	17	18	19	20	21	22	23	24	25	26	27	28	29	30	31	32	33	34	35	36
recognise, find and name a half as one of two equal parts of an object, shape or quantity																		•	•	•																
recognise, find and name a quarter as one of four equal parts of an object, shape or quantity																		•	•	•																

Notes and guidance (non-statutory)

	1	2	3	4	5	6	7	8	9	10	11	12	13	14	15	16	17	18	19	20	21	22	23	24	25	26	27	28	29	30	31	32	33	34	35	36
Pupils are taught half and quarter as 'fractions of' discrete and continuous quantities by solving problems using shapes, objects and quantities. For example, they could recognise and find half a length, quantity, set of objects or shape. Pupils connect halves and quarters to the equal sharing and grouping of sets of objects and to measures, as well as recognising and combining halves and quarters as parts of a whole.																		•	•	•																

Stretch and Challenge Issue

Measurement

Measurement	1	2	3	4	5	6	7	8	9	10	11	12	13	14	15	16	17	18	19	20	21	22	23	24	25	26	27	28	29	30	31	32	33	34	35	36
• compare, describe and solve practical problems for: – lengths and heights [for example, long/short, longer/shorter, tall/short, double/half] – mass/weight [for example, heavy/light, heavier than, lighter than] – capacity and volume [for example, full/empty, more than, less than, half, half full, quarter] – time [for example, quicker, slower, earlier, later]																						•	•	•	•	•	•									
• measure and begin to record the following: – lengths and heights – mass/weight – capacity and volume – time (hours, minutes, seconds)																						•	•	•	•	•	•									
• recognise and know the value of different denominations of coins and notes				•	•	•	•	•	•	•	•	•	•	•	•	•	•	•	•								•									
• sequence events in chronological order using language [for example, before and after, next, first, today, yesterday, tomorrow, morning, afternoon and evening]																									•	•	•									
• recognise and use language relating to dates, including days of the week, weeks, months and years																									•	•	•									
• tell the time to the hour and half past the hour and draw the hands on a clock face to show these times																									•											

Stretch and Challenge Issue

Measurement Continued

Notes and guidance (non-statutory)

	1	2	3	4	5	6	7	8	9	10	11	12	13	14	15	16	17	18	19	20	21	22	23	24	25	26	27	28	29	30	31	32	33	34	35	36
The pairs of terms: mass and weight, volume and capacity, are used interchangeably at this stage.																					•		•		•		•									
Pupils move from using and comparing different types of quantities and measures using non-standard units, including discrete (for example, counting) and continuous (for example, liquid) measurement, to using manageable common standard units.																					•		•		•		•									
In order to become familiar with standard measures, pupils begin to use measuring tools such as a ruler, weighing scales and containers.																					•		•		•		•									
Pupils use the language of time, including telling the time throughout the day, first using o'clock and then half past.																									•		•									

Geometry – Properties of shapes

- recognise and name common 2-D and 3-D shapes, including:
  - 2-D shapes [for example, rectangles (including squares), circles and triangles]
  - 3-D shapes [for example, cuboids (including cubes), pyramids and spheres]

	1	2	3	4	5	6	7	8	9	10	11	12	13	14	15	16	17	18	19	20	21	22	23	24	25	26	27	28	29	30	31	32	33	34	35	36
recognise and name common 2-D and 3-D shapes																												•		•		•				

Notes and guidance (non-statutory)

	1	2	3	4	5	6	7	8	9	10	11	12	13	14	15	16	17	18	19	20	21	22	23	24	25	26	27	28	29	30	31	32	33	34	35	36
Pupils handle common 2-D and 3-D shapes, naming these and related everyday objects fluently. They recognise these shapes in different orientations and sizes, and know that rectangles, triangles, cuboids and pyramids are not always similar to each other.																												•		•		•				

Stretch and Challenge Issue

	1	2	3	4	5	6	7	8	9	10	11	12	13	14	15	16	17	18	19	20	21	22	23	24	25	26	27	28	29	30	31	32	33	34	35	36
Geometry – Position and direction																																				
• describe position, direction and movement, including whole, half, quarter and three-quarter turns																															•	•	•	•		
Notes and guidance (non-statutory)																																				
Pupils use the language of position, direction and motion, including: left and right, top, middle and bottom, on top of, in front of, above, between, around, near, close and far, up and down, forwards and backwards, inside and outside.																															•	•	•	•		
Pupils make whole, half, quarter and three-quarter turns in both directions and connect turning clockwise with movement on a clock face.																																•	•	•		

Cross-curricular links to the National Curriculum Programme of Study

Cross-curricular link and *Stretch and Challenge* Feature

Domain(s)	Topic	Issue	What's the Problem?	Looking for Patterns	The Puzzler	Let's Investigate	The Language of Maths	Focus on Science	Technology Today	Around the World	In the Past	The Arts Roundup	Construct	Sports Update	Money Matters	At Home
			Mathematics				**English**	**Science**	**Computing**	**Geography**	**History**	**Art & Design / Music**	**Design & Technology**	**Physical Education**	**Links to money**	**Links with home**
Number: – Number and place value	Number	1		•	•	•	•									
	Number	2		•		•	•									
	Number	3		•	•	•	•							•		
	Number	4		•	•	•			•							
Number: – Addition and subtraction	Addition	5			•	•									•	
	Addition	6		•	•	•								•	•	
	Subtraction	7	•		•							•				
	Subtraction	8		•	•	•										
Number: – Multiplication and division	Multiplication	9	•	•		•									•	•
	Multiplication	10	•			•	•									
	Division	11	•	•		•									•	
	Division	12	•			•	•								•	
Number: – Mixed operations – Addition and subtraction	Mixed operations	13		•	•	•				•					•	
	Mixed operations	14		•	•										•	
Number: – Multiplication and division	Mixed operations	15		•		•			•						•	
	Mixed operations	16			•	•									•	
	Mixed operations	17		•		•									•	
	Mixed operations	18	•	•	•	•			•					•		

17

Cross-curricular link and *Stretch and Challenge Feature*

Feature	Category	19	20	21	22	23	24	25	26	27	28	29	30	31	32	33	34	35	36
At Home	Links with home				•	•	•	•	•	•		•		•				•	•
Money Matters	Links to money		•	•						•									
Sports Update	Physical Education																		
Construct	Design & Technology		•							•	•	•	•	•			•		
The Arts Roundup	Art & Design / Music		•																
In the Past	History										•								
Around the World	Geography				•														
Technology Today	Computing																		
Focus on Science	Science	•			•	•	•		•	•								•	•
The Language of Maths	English			•			•	•		•		•		•	•	•	•	•	•
Let's Investigate	Mathematics	•	•	•	•	•	•	•	•		•	•	•					•	•
The Puzzler	Mathematics	•	•	•	•						•			•	•	•	•		
Looking for Patterns	Mathematics	•				•			•		•	•	•		•	•	•		
What's the Problem?	Mathematics	•		•				•											
Issue		19	20	21	22	23	24	25	26	27	28	29	30	31	32	33	34	35	36
Topic		Fractions	Fractions	Fractions	Length and height	Weight and mass	Capacity and volume	Time	Measurement	Measurement	2-D shapes	3-D shapes	Patterns	Position and direction	Movement	Geometry	Geometry	Statistics	Statistics
Domain(s)		Number: – Fractions			Measurement						Geometry: – Properties of shapes			Geometry: – Position and direction		Geometry: – Properties of shapes – Position and direction		Statistics	

Resources used in *Stretch and Challenge 1*

A fundamental skill of mathematics is knowing what resources to use and when it is appropriate to use them. It is for this reason that many of the activities in *Stretch and Challenge* give no indication to the children as to which resources to use. Although the teacher's notes that accompany each activity include a list of resources, children should be encouraged to work out for themselves what they will need to use to successfully complete an activity.

It is assumed that for each activity children will have ready access to pencil and paper, and any other resources that are specifically mentioned in an activity, for example, computers or other Resource sheets. However, all other equipment should be left for the children to locate and use as and when they see is appropriate.

A list of all the resources children are likely to need in *Stretch and Challenge 1* is given below.

Resource	Stretch and Challenge Issue																	
	1	2	3	4	5	6	7	8	9	10	11	12	13	14	15	16	17	18
pencil and paper	•	•	•	•	•	•	•	•	•	•	•	•	•	•	•	•	•	•
Resource sheet	2, 3	2, 3, 4	2, 3, 5	2, 3, 6	2, 3	2, 3	2, 3	2, 3	2, 3, 7, 19	2, 3, 19	2, 3, 7	2, 3	2, 3	2, 3	2, 3	2, 3	2, 3, 6	2, 3, 6
ruler									•									
scissors				•					•		•					•	•	
glue				•												•	•	
calculator				•		•						•			•			
counters				•	•		•	•	•	•	•	•		•		•		
interlocking cubes	•				•						•							
1–100 number square				•														
Tens and Ones abacus and beads	•	•																
large sheet of paper				•													•	
0–9 digit cards		•		•						•		•			•			
1–20 number cards		•																
1–50 number cards		•																
coloured pencils					•				•				•					
A4 paper																		
pencil and paper clip (for a spinner)											•							
0–9 dice					•									•				
1p, 2p, 5p and 10p coins						•												
double-5 dominoes							•											
container							•											
double-6 dominoes								•										
1–6 dice								•		•			•			•		
buttons										•	•							
Compare Bears (or similar)											•							
5p, 10p, 20p, 50p, £1 and £2 coins											•							
£1 coins																		
5p, 10p and 20p coins													•					
+, –, and = operator cards																	•	
1p, 2p, 5p, 10p, 20p, 50p and £1 coins																	•	

Resource	Stretch and Challenge Issue																	
	19	20	21	22	23	24	25	26	27	28	29	30	31	32	33	34	35	36
pencil and paper	•	•	•	•	•	•	•	•	•	•	•	•	•	•	•	•	•	•
Resource sheet	2, 3, 8	2, 3, 9	2, 3	2, 3	2, 3	2, 3	2, 3, 10	2, 3, 6	2, 3	2, 3, 11–13, 19	2, 3, 14	2, 3, 15, 16, 19	2, 3, 7	2, 3	2, 3, 17, 19	2, 3, 20	2, 3	2, 3
ruler	•			•						•	•	•			•	•		
scissors						•			•		•	•		•		•		
glue									•			•		•				
calculator											•							
counters			•									•		•				
interlocking cubes		•		•			•		•		•				•			
+, −, and = operator cards																		
1p, 2p, 5p, 10p, 20p, 50p and £1 coins														•				
large sheet of paper																		
0–9 digit cards																		
coloured pencils	•	•	•								•	•	•	•	•	•	•	•
large box; 3-D geometric shapes, including a large number of rectangular and triangular prisms; large sheet of paper; drawing materials											•							
A4 paper		•											•					
small Compare Bears (or similar)														•				
1–6 dice				•										•				•
selection of 2-D shapes; Lego; selection of 3-D shapes															•			
sheet of coloured square paper; geoboard; elastic bands																•		
string or wool					•													
scale balance; measuring scales; book; 1 kg weight; 0–9 dice; spoon; more than 1 kg of rice; more than 1 kg of pasta or sugar or flour						•												
collection of small objects such as marbles, cubes, paper clips, pasta shells; access to a tap; bowl; 1 litre measuring jug; matchbox; large bottle of mineral water or fizzy drink; paper cups; collection of small containers such as yoghurt pot, paper cup, egg cup, paint pot; material for making a poster, such as large sheet of paper, colouring materials, magazines						•												
stopwatch or clock with a seconds hand							•											
collection of different sized containers; measuring jug; access to water; ice cube tray; salt; sugar; fruit juice; fizzy drink								•										
wooden beads; laces or string; measuring scales; paintbrush; collection of different sponges; access to water; large bowl; measuring jug									•									
£1 coins				•														

S&C Volume 1

The Maths Herald

Name:

Date:

Looking for Patterns

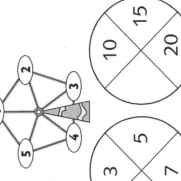

Follow the patterns to find the missing numbers.

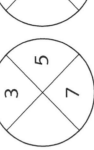

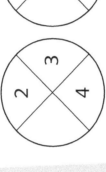

Let's Investigate

0, 1, 2, 3, 4, 5, 6, 7, 8, 9

The number 15 is made using two digits: 1 and 5.
How many digits are there altogether on a 0–20 number track?

1	2	3	4	5	6	7	8	9	10	11	12	13	14	15	16	17	18	19	20

The Puzzler

One hand in each row is different.

Draw a ring around this hand.

Let's Investigate

This abacus shows the number 14.

If you add 1 bead to the abacus you can make the numbers 15 or 24.

What numbers can you make by adding 1 bead to these abacus?

and

and

and

and

and

and

Let's Investigate

This abacus shows the number 24 using 6 beads.

Write all the numbers you can make on an abacus using 6 beads.

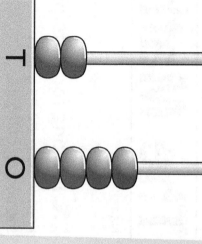

Looking for Patterns

This shape is made from interlocking cubes. Each side is 3 cubes long.

How many cubes are there altogether?

Make a shape like this with sides 4 cubes long.

How many cubes are there altogether?

What about for shapes with sides 5, 6, 7, … cubes long?

What patterns do you notice?

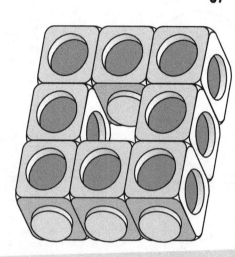

place value

Looking for Patterns

14   16   13   27   11
9   17   37   31   32
7   51   8   42   11
41   5   2

Use the numbers above to complete each number pattern.

23   20   [ ]   [ ]   5   2

2   7   12   17   22

91   81   71   [ ]   21   11   1

[ ]   15   17   19   21   23

The Language of Maths

Think of a number between 0 and 50.

Make up 3 clues about your number.

Can a friend guess your number?

S&C Volume 1

The Maths Herald

Name:

Date:

Let's Investigate

Choose any 3 digit cards.

How many different 2-digit numbers can you make?

We're a 2-digit number.

| 1 | 2 | 3 | 4 | 5 | 6 | 7 | 8 | 9 |

Looking for Patterns

If you wrote all the numbers from 1 to 50, how many times would you write the 4 digit? Guess first. Then check.

digit

20 21 22 23 21

The Language of Maths

Play this game with a friend.

- Each player secretly chooses 1 of the cards and puts it face down beside them.
- Take turns to ask questions about your friend's number. Use the rules on the flags to help.
- The first player to guess their friend's number wins.
- Play 5 rounds.

You need:
- a set of 1–20 number cards

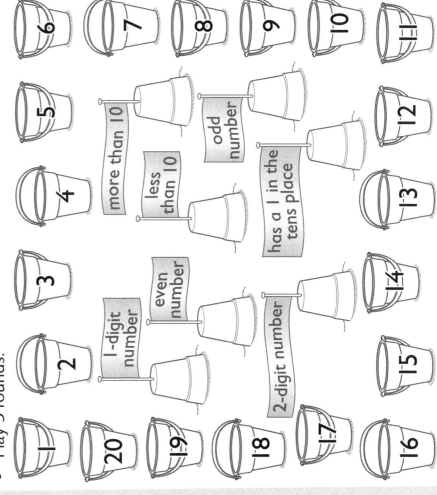

more than 10

less than 10

odd number

even number

has a 1 in the tens place

1-digit number

2-digit number

1 2 3 4 5 6 7 8 9 10 11 12 13 14 15 16 17 18 19 20

Looking for Patterns

Start at 0. Jump on in steps of 2. Write the numbers you land on.

Start at 0. Jump on in steps of 3. Write the numbers you land on.

Start at 0. Jump on in steps of 4. Write the numbers you land on.

Start at 0. Jump on in steps of 5. Write the numbers you land on.

Let's Investigate

This abacus shows the number 15.

If you subtract 1 bead from the abacus you can make the numbers 14 or 5.

What numbers can you make by subtracting 1 bead from these abacus?

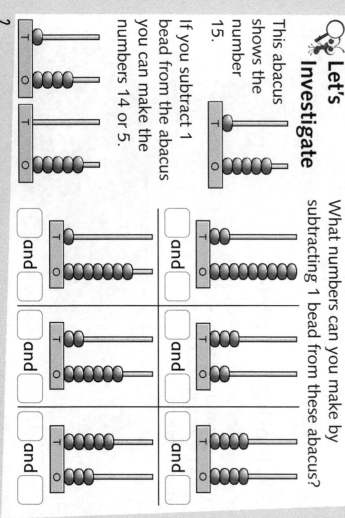

and	and	and
and	and	and

Looking for Patterns

Write the next 3 numbers in each pattern.

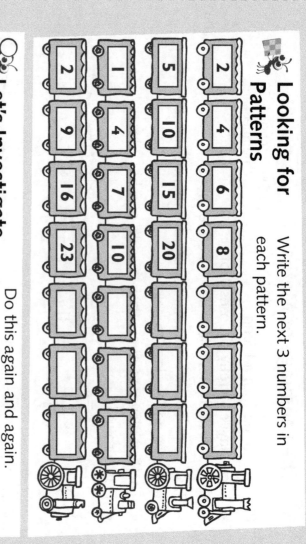

2 4 6 8

5 10 15 20

1 4 7 10

2 9 16 23

Do this again and again.
Then answer these questions:

• When does an even number stay even?

• When does an even number become an odd number?

• When does an odd number stay an odd number?

• When does an odd number become an even number?

Let's Investigate

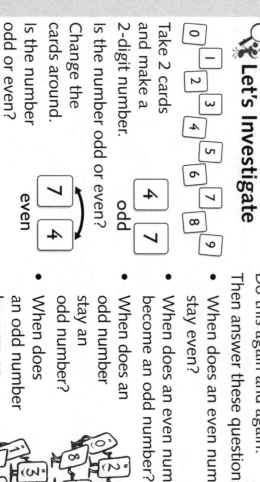

0 1 2 3 4 5 6 7 8 9

Take 2 cards and make a 2-digit number.

Is the number odd or even?

[4] [7]   odd

Change the cards around.

Is the number odd or even?

[7] [4]   even

Put the cards back.

Choose another 2 cards and do the same thing.

The Maths Herald

Name:

Date:

Looking for Patterns

Count on and back in ones.

Count on → 0 ... Count back → 10

Count on and back in twos.

Count on → 0 ... Count back → 20

Count on and back in tens.

Count on → 0 ... Count back → 100

What do you notice about the number you wrote in each of the 3 large shapes?

Let's Investigate

A car has 4 wheels.
A motorbike has 2 wheels.
Mike counts 12 wheels.
What did Mike see?

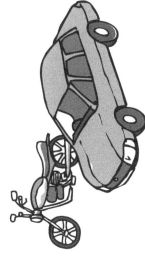

The Language of Maths

1 2 3 4 5 6 7 8 9

Write the digits 1 to 9 in any order in the grid.

A	B	C
D	E	F
G	H	I

Now on the sheet, write some clues just like in The Puzzler.

When you have written all your clues, give your sheet to a friend.

When your friend has finished, compare your grid with your friend's.

Are they the same? If not, find out why.

The Puzzler

1 2 3 4 5 6 7 8 9

Use the clues to write the digits 1 to 9 in the grid.

A: This digit is odd.

B: This digit is less than 2.

C: This digit is half of 12.

D: This digit is 1 more than E.

E: This digit is the answer to 3 + 4.

F: This digit is 2 more than B.

G: This digit is between 1 and 3.

H: This digit is even.

I: This is the largest digit.

A	B	C
D	E	F
G	H	I

Looking for Patterns

These numbers belong in the patterns.

Write each number in the correct pattern.

3	6	9	12
4	8	12	16
2	5	8	11
1	6	11	16
3	9	15	21

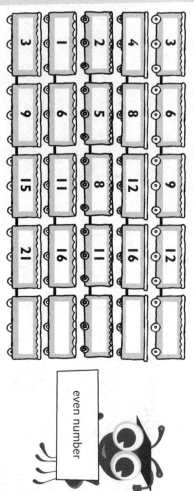

14	20	27	15	21

even number

Sports Update

Lee, Mark, Amy and Josh all play on the same football team.

They wear the numbers 1, 2, 3 and 4.

Use the clues to work out which player wears which number.

Draw lines to match the player with their number.

1. Lee's number is between 2 and 4.
2. Mark's number is even.
3. Josh's number is the largest.
4. One of the girls is number 1.

Lee   Josh   Amy   Mark

1   2   3   4

Looking for Patterns

Continue the patterns.

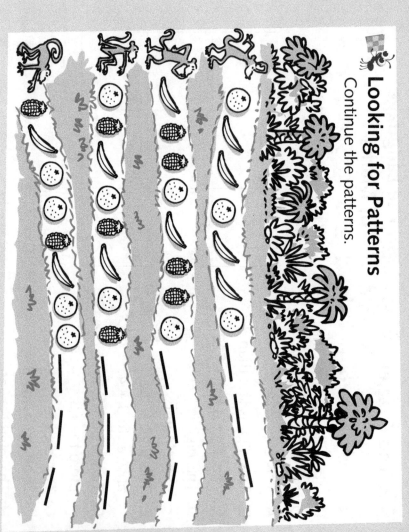

The Puzzler

Simon built a fire.

He put the logs on the fire one at a time.

Label the logs 1st, 2nd, 3rd, 4th and 5th to show how Simon built the fire.

The Maths Herald

Name:

Date:

Looking for Patterns

Cut out the pictures of dogs, cats and chickens.

2 dogs, 2 cats and 2 chickens go for a walk along a narrow path.

Show 2 dogs, 2 cats and 2 chickens going for a walk in a different order.

Keep doing this until you have used all your animals.

Technology Today

Investigate making different patterns using a calculator.

Here are 2 to get you started.

Looking for Patterns

Here are 5 cards from a set of 0–9 digit cards.

The cards are in order smallest to largest but only the 6 digit card is showing.

| | | 6 | | |

The cards could be:

| 0 | 4 | 7 | 9 | or | 1 | 3 | 6 | 8 | 9 |

Write down what other numbers the cards could be.

Looking for Patterns

If I start at 5 and count on in fives I will say the number 100.

If I start at 32 and count back in twos I will say the number 13.

Is Sunita correct? Explain your reasoning.

Is Connor correct? Explain your reasoning.

Looking for Patterns

Work out the number in the box.

5 → [ ] → [10] → 10

10 → [40] → 11

3 → [ ] → 11

6 → [ ] → [ ] → 14

2 → 22

4 → [ ] → 19

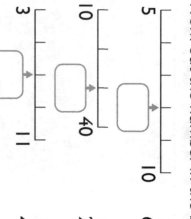
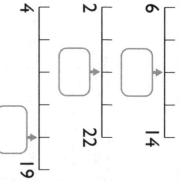
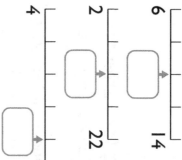
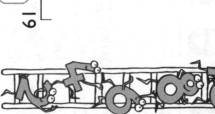

The Puzzler

Players in a 5-a-side team wear one of these numbers on their kit:

1, 2, 3, 4 or 5.

The players of a 5-a-side team are waiting for their lunch.

Use the clues to work out in which order the players are standing.

1. Number 3 is in the middle.
2. The smallest number is at the end.
3. An even number is at the start.
4. Number 4 is after Number 2.
5. Number 5 is between Numbers 3 and 1.

Looking for Patterns

Gavin is stacking cans in a supermarket.

He has finished when there is just 1 can on top.

How many more cans does Gavin need to add?

How many cans will there be altogether?

Let's Investigate

People have 1 head and 2 legs.

Dogs have 1 head and 4 legs.

Toby counts 4 heads.
What does Toby see?
How many legs does Toby see?

divide

S&C Volume 1

The Maths Herald

Name:

Date:

Money Matters

Look at teddy.

Work out a price for the different parts of teddy's body.

How much does teddy cost altogether?

The Puzzler

1, 2, 3, 4, 5

Write each of the numbers 1 to 5 in the boxes so that each line adds up to 8.

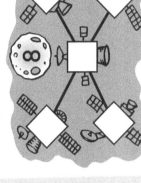

Write each of the numbers 1 to 5 in the boxes so that each line adds up to 9.

Let's Investigate

How many different ways can you put 10 counters into these 3 bags?

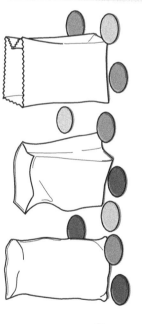

Let's Investigate

You need:
• 0–9 dice

Roll the dice and write the number in one of the shapes above. Do this until each shape has a number written in it.

Now use the numbers in the shapes above to work out the answers to these number sentences.

Try and make some different number sentences using the numbers in the shapes.

What about subtraction number sentences?

Let's Investigate

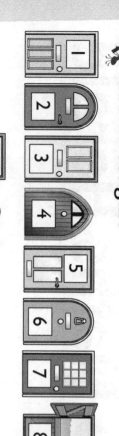

The numbers 3 4 are next-door numbers.

The total of 3 and 4 is 7.   3 + 4 = 7

Choose other pairs of next-door numbers and add them together.

Write about what you notice.

total

The Puzzler

In this grid, the total of each row ↔ and column ↕ is written in the circles ◯.

Complete these grids.

7	9
6	3

◯ ◯
◯

4	10
13	7

◯ ◯
◯

3	5
6	7

⑨ ⑫
⑧ ⑬

12	11
8	6

◯ ◯
◯

The Puzzler

In these grids, the total of each row ↔ and column ↕ is written in the circles ◯.

Write the numbers that belong in the boxes.

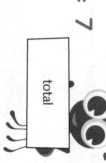

⑥ ⑤
③ ⑧

⑦ ⑤
⑤ ⑦

④ ⑨
⑧ ⑤

The Puzzler

The numbers around the star all add up to the number in the middle.

Write the missing numbers on the stars.

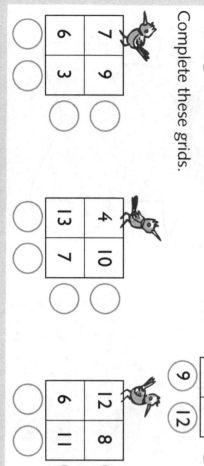

The Maths Herald

Name:

Date:

Sports Update

  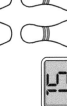  

7 2 6 3 5
    4

Tammy scored

8 POINTS

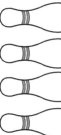

3 5

by knocking down the

Which skittles did she knock down to score these points?

14 POINTS

15 POINTS

11 POINTS

6 POINTS

12 POINTS

10 POINTS

Let's Investigate

Jake takes 12 cubes.

He arranges them to make this flat shape.

> This shape has a row of 2 cubes, a row of 3 cubes, a row of 4 cubes and another row of 3 cubes.

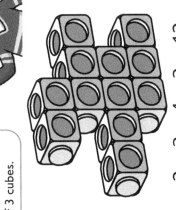

How many different flat shapes can you make using 12 cubes?

Write a number sentence for each shape.

$2 + 3 + 4 + 3 = 12$

The Puzzler

1, 2, 3, 4, 5, 6, 7

Write each of the numbers 1 to 7 on the circles so that each line adds to 12.

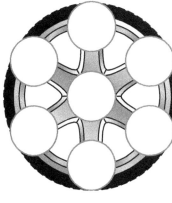

12

Write each of the numbers 1 to 7 on the circles so that each line adds to 10.

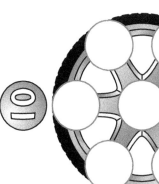

10

Let's Investigate

Take 10 cubes and make a rod.

Now break your rod in two.

Place 1 piece on each hand.

Write a number sentence to explain how many cubes are in each hand.

Now put the 2 pieces back together.

Find different ways to break your rod in 2.

Write a number sentence each time.

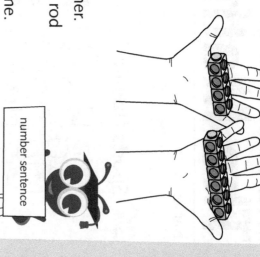

number sentence

Sports Update

The numbers on the sports kit in each team must add up to 25. Use these numbers to complete the teams.

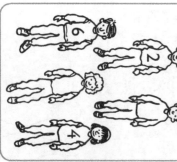

4 5 6 7 8 9

Money Matters

Using 4 1p coins, 4 2p coins, 4 5p coins and 4 10p coins, make each row ←→, column ↕ and diagonal ↘ ↙ total 18p.

Sports Update

Hop down this square. Begin at the START line and hop to the FINISH line. You cannot go backwards or sideways. Add up the numbers you land on.

START

4	2	1	6	3
5	3	7	8	4
7	9	5	6	8
2	8	7	4	1
7	1	3	5	2

FINISH

Here is one route.

Draw in the route that scores the most points.

What is your total?

Use a different colour. Draw in the route that scores the least points.

What is your total?

4	2	1	6	3
5	3	7	8	4
7	9	5	6	8
2	8	7	4	1
7	1	3	5	2

S&C Volume 1

The Maths Herald

Name:

Date:

Looking for Patterns

There is a difference of 3 where these two dominoes touch.

Use 7 dominoes to complete this chain. Make sure touching dominoes have a difference of 3.

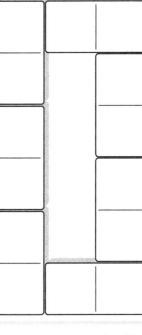

The Arts Roundup

Louis is a painter.

He is having a two day show to sell his paintings.

He starts with 16 paintings.

On the 1st day he sells 7 paintings.

On the 2nd day he sells 5 paintings.

How many paintings did Louis not sell?

The Puzzler

Play this game with a friend.

- Place the 20 counters in a pile.
- Decide who starts.
- Take turns to take away 1 or 2 counters and put them in the container.
- The winner is the player who puts the last counter in the container.

Play the game several times.

When you have played the game a few times, talk about ways of winning the game.

You need:
- 20 counters
- container

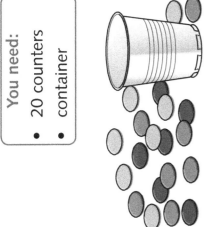

What's the Problem?

Look at Karen's homework.

All her answers are right except one.

Which one did she get wrong?

Why?

What is the right answer?

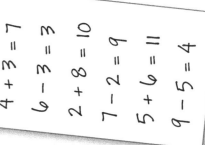

$4 + 3 = 7$

$6 - 3 = 3$

$2 + 8 = 10$

$7 - 2 = 9$

$5 + 6 = 11$

$9 - 5 = 4$

The Puzzler

Before   After

$6 - 4 = 2$

Write a number sentence for each pair of hourglasses.

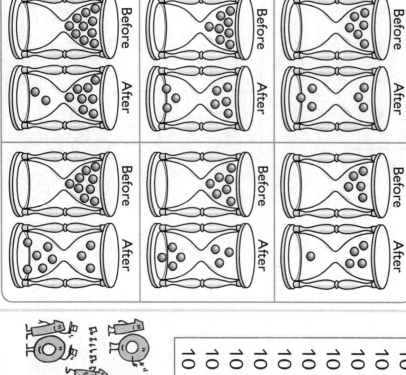

Before   After

Before   After

Before   After

Before   After

Before   After

Before   After

Looking for Patterns

Look at these subtraction number facts for 10.

What patterns do you notice?

$10 - 0 = 10$
$10 - 1 = 9$
$10 - 2 = 8$
$10 - 3 = 7$
$10 - 4 = 6$
$10 - 5 = 5$
$10 - 6 = 4$
$10 - 7 = 3$
$10 - 8 = 2$
$10 - 9 = 1$
$10 - 10 = 0$

The Puzzler

Look at the hourglasses in The Puzzler activity on page 2.

Now write a number sentence for each of these hourglasses.

subtract

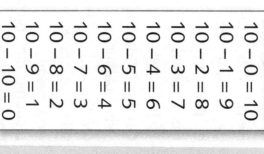

After   After

After   After

After   After

The Puzzler

Subtract the numbers on the balls from the number on the lorry.
Write the answer underneath.

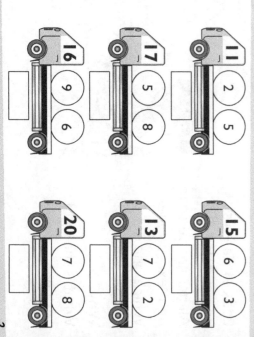

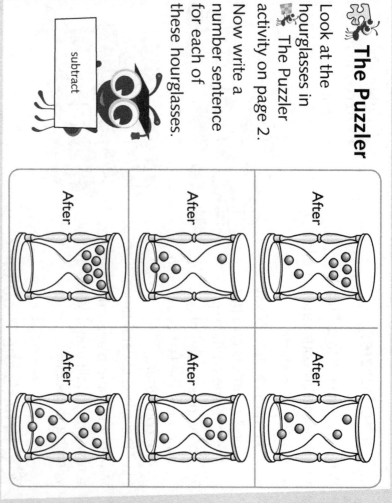

11   2   5
17   5   8
16   9   6
15   6   3
13   7   2
20   7   8

The Maths Herald

Name:

Date:

The Puzzler

Find the difference between the number on the balloon and the number on the dart.

Write the answer on the box underneath.

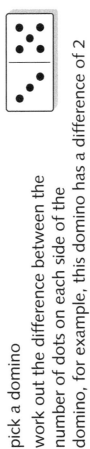

The Puzzler

Find pairs of numbers that are next to each other, like this ⬚ or like this ⬚ with a difference of 3.

Draw a ring around them. One has been done for you.

Colour in pairs of numbers that are next to each other, like this ▨ or like this ▨▨ , with a difference of 6.

One number does not have a ring around it and is not coloured in.

Which number is this?

10	4	15	21
8	9	7	13
2	12	9	17
6	5	10	14
9	11	13	16

The Puzzler

Play this game with a friend.

You need:
- set of dominoes
- 14 counters – 7 of one colour, 7 of another colour

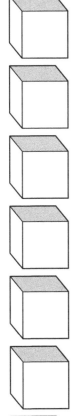

Before you start:
- look at the domino differences you wrote in the second 🔍 Let's Investigate activity on page 3. Write each of these numbers on one of the boxes above
- spread the dominoes face down on the table
- decide who will have which colour counters.

Take turns to:
- pick a domino
- work out the difference between the number of dots on each side of the domino, for example, this domino has a difference of 2

- put one of your counters on the box that has this number. If there is already one of your counters on the box, you miss a turn.

The winner is the first player to put a counter on all of the boxes. If the dominoes run out first, the player with more counters on the boxes wins.

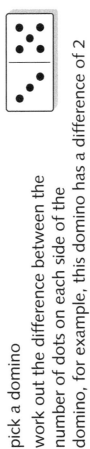

Let's Investigate

This box means that you need to find 2 squares next to each other on the grid that have a difference of 9.

9	

Find these pairs of numbers on the grid.

10	

2			4	11

7	6

6	

8	10	1	3
14	5	12	7
9	15	6	13
4	11	0	2

Let's Investigate

Look at the grid in the Let's Investigate activity opposite.

These pairs of numbers all have a difference of 5.

5	12	7

5	10	**5**
5	14	**5**
5	9	**5**

5	10	5
5	9	4

Find all the pairs of numbers on the grid that have a difference of 9.

difference

Let's Investigate

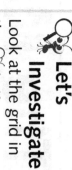

What are all the possible differences between two 1–6 dice?

Write them here.

[blank box]

You need:
- two 1–6 dice

The difference between these two dice is 2.

5 – 3 = 2

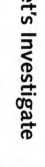

Let's Investigate

An activity to do with a friend.

What are all the possible differences between the numbers of dots on a set of dominoes?

Write them here.

[blank box]

You need:
- set of dominoes

The difference between the numbers of dots on each side of this domino is 4.

6 – 2 = 4

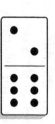

The Maths Herald

Name:

Date:

Looking for Patterns

How many fingers do you have on both hands?

Altogether how many fingers do you and a friend have?

What about 3, 4, 5, 6, … children?

What patterns do you notice?

Looking for Patterns

How many arms and legs do you have?

Altogether how many arms and legs do you and a friend have?

What about 3, 4, 5, 6, … children?

What patterns do you notice?

Let's Investigate

Look at the sheet.

Put 1 counter on each shelf. How many counters have you used?

Put another counter on each shelf. How many counters are there now?

Keep adding a counter to each shelf. Write down how many counters there are each time.

How many counters can you put in your cupboard?

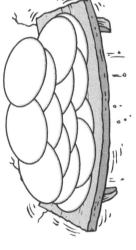

Money Matters

If the value of the shaded part is 5p, then the total value of the shape is 20p.

What is the total value of each of these shapes?

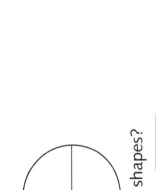

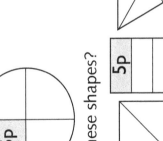

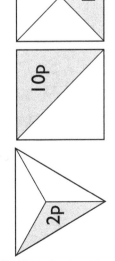

10p

1p

5p

10p

2p

Let's Investigate

Tim cut up a sheet of squared paper into different sized rectangles.

For each rectangle he then drew a cross in each square.

This is how he described this rectangle.

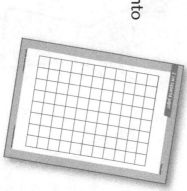

5 columns of 2 is 10.
5 lots of 2 is 10.

2 rows of 5 is 10.
2 lots of 5 is 10.

Take a sheet of squared paper and cut it into different sized rectangles.

Then, like Tim, describe each of your rectangles.

What's the Problem?

This bird has 5 spots on each wing. How many spots does it have altogether?

How many spots do these birds have altogether?

Looking for Patterns

Altogether how many fingers and toes do you have?

How many fingers and toes do you and a friend have?

What about 3, 4, 5, 6, …
children?

What patterns do you notice?

At Home

How many people are in your family?

Remember to count yourself.

How many feet are there in your family altogether?

How many toes is this?

If you have any animals in your home, how many feet is this altogether?

S&C Volume 1

The Maths Herald

Name:

Date:

3 lots of 4 is 12

4 lots of 3 is 12

Let's Investigate

Place counters onto the squares on a sheet of squared paper to make different sized rectangles.

Then, like Fiona, describe each of your rectangles.

multiply

What's the Problem?

Mrs Giles has 7 hens.

Each hen lays 5 eggs in a week.

How many eggs does Mrs Giles get in one week?

How many eggs does 1 hen lay in 5 weeks?

Mrs Giles buys 4 more hens.

How many eggs does she get in 1 week now?

Looking for Patterns

Play this game with a friend.

You need:
- 1–6 dice
- some counters
- 2 buttons

- Before you start, work together to put a counter on all the multiples of 5.

- Take turns to:
  – roll the dice and move your button that number of spaces
  – if you land on a multiple of 5, take the counter.

- The game ends when one player reaches the star.

- The winner is the player with more counters.

1	2	3	4	5	6	7	8	9	10
36	37	38	39	40	41	42	43	44	11
35	64	65	66	67	68	69	70	45	12
34	63	84	85	86	87	88	71	46	13
33	62	83	96	97	98	89	72	47	14
32	61	82	95	100	99	90	73	48	15
31	60	81	94	93	92	91	74	49	16
30	59	80	79	78	77	76	75	50	17
29	58	57	56	55	54	53	52	51	18
28	27	26	25	24	23	22	21	20	19

The Language of Maths

2, 4, 6, 8, 10, 12, ☐, ☐, ☐, ☐

These numbers are **multiples of 2**.

2 will divide exactly into each number.

5, 10, 15, 20, 25, 30, ☐, ☐, ☐, ☐

These numbers are **multiples of 5**.

5 will divide exactly into each number.

10, 20, 30, 40, 50, 60, ☐, ☐, ☐, ☐

These numbers are **multiples of 10**.

10 will divide exactly into each number.

Write the next 4 multiples of 2, 5 and 10.

Can you write the next
5 multiples of 3?

What about the next
5 multiples of 4?

3, ☐, ☐, ☐, ☐

4, ☐, ☐, ☐, ☐

What's the Problem?

There are 5 sheep and 7 chickens in the farmyard.

How many legs are there in the farmyard?

Looking for Patterns

Continue each of these number patterns.

2, 4, 6, 8, ...

45, 40, 35, 30, ...

9, 12, 15, 18, ...

27, 25, 23, ...

20, 30, 50, 80, ...

15, ...

Looking for Patterns

Look at this 1–100 number square.

Some of the multiples of 2 have a cross ✗ through them.

Some of the multiples of 5 have a ring ◯ around them.

One of the multiples of 10 is shaded ▮.

Continue the patterns. What do you notice?

1	2	3	4	5	6	7	8	9	10
11	12	13	14	15	16	17	18	19	20
21	22	23	24	25	26	27	28	29	30
31	32	33	34	35	36	37	38	39	40
41	42	43	44	45	46	47	48	49	50
51	52	53	54	55	56	57	58	59	60
61	62	63	64	65	66	67	68	69	70
71	72	73	74	75	76	77	78	79	80
81	82	83	84	85	86	87	88	89	90
91	92	93	94	95	96	97	98	99	100

The Maths Herald

Name:

Date:

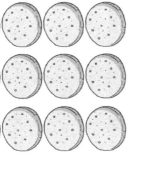

🐜 What's the Problem?

Jake, Lisa and their mum bake a tray of biscuits.

If the biscuits are shared between Jake, Lisa and their mum, how many will they each get?

If the biscuits are shared only between Jake and Lisa, how many will they each get?

Jake and Lisa each invite a friend over to play, if they share the biscuits between all 4 of them how many will they each get?

🐜 Let's Investigate

| 1 | 2 | 3 | 4 |

Using the digit cards 1, 2, 3 and 4, put 2 cards together to make a 2 digit number.

| 2 | 4 |

You can make 12 different two-digit numbers using these 4 digit cards. What are they?

Which numbers can be divided exactly by 2?

Which numbers can be divided exactly by 3?

Which numbers can be divided exactly by 4?

🐜 What's the Problem?

I have more than 12 CDs, but less than 20. When I put the CDs into groups of 2, I have 1 left over. When I put them into groups of 3, I have 2 left over.

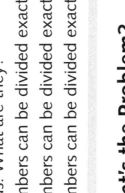

How many CDs does Lisa have?

Let's Investigate

Look at the sheet.

Cut out the toys at the bottom of the sheet.

- How many toys are there?

- Put all the toys onto 2 shelves. Put the same number of toys on each shelf.

How many toys are on each shelf?

Take the toys off the shelves.

- Now put them all onto 3 shelves. Put the same number of toys on each shelf.

How many toys are on each shelf?

Take the toys off the shelves.

- Now put them all onto 4 shelves. Put the same number on each shelf.

How many toys are on each shelf?

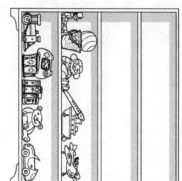

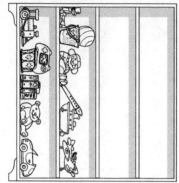

What's the Problem?

12 bears are going on a picnic. They travel in groups of 2.

How many groups travel to the picnic?

What other ways could they divide into equal sized groups to travel to the picnic?

How many groups is this each time?

Let's Investigate

One lily pad can hold 5 frogs. Any more frogs and the lily pad sinks.

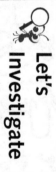

Draw the number of lily pads needed to hold this many frogs.

| 15 frogs | 25 frogs |
| 33 frogs | 37 frogs |

Money Matters

How many make ?

How many make ?

How many make ?

How many make ?

How many make ?

How many make ?

How many make ?

How many make ?

© HarperCollins Publishers 2016

S&C Volume 1

The Maths Herald

Name:

Date:

Let's Investigate

Make a rod of 16 cubes.

How many different ways can you find to split these 16 cubes into towers all the same height?

How many towers are there?

How many cubes are there in each tower?

What if you used 20 cubes or 24 cubes?

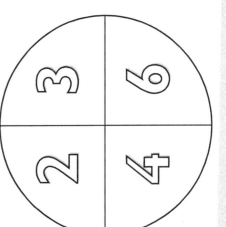

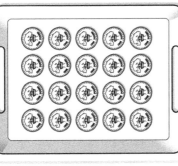

Money Matters

Some friends win this money.

They decide to share the money equally between all of them.

How many friends might have won the money?

How much money would they each get?

The Language of Maths

Play this game with a friend.

You need:
- 24 counters
- pencil
- paper clip
- 12 buttons

- Before you start, take 12 counters each.

- Take turns to:

  – spin the spinner

  – divide your 12 counters into this number of groups – each group must have the same number of counters in it.

- The player with more counters in each of their groups wins the round and takes a button.

- If you both have the same number in each group, you both take a button.

- The first player to collect 6 buttons wins the game.

What's the Problem?

42 divided by 6 is …

How might Leroy work out the answer to this number sentence?

2   3
4   6

Let's Investigate

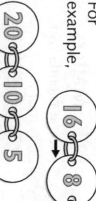

Start with any even number less than 50.

Keep halving this number until you reach an odd number.

For example,

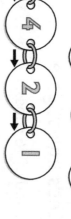

20 → 10 → 5

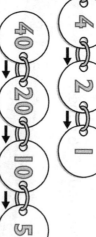

16 → 8 → 4 → 2 → 1

40 → 20 → 10 → 5

The number 16 is the longest of these number chains.

What is the longest number chain you can find?

 30
48 12 8
 22 32 10
 38 24 26 44

Looking for Patterns

Divide each of these numbers by 10.

What do you notice about your answers?

 40
 50
80
30
90
60

You can use a calculator if you need to.

Let's Investigate

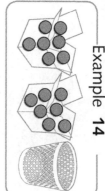

Choose any number between 10 and 30.

Take that many counters.

Divide the counters between the 2 boxes so that there are the same number of counters in each box.

Example 14

Example 17

If there are any counters left over, put them into the bin.

Which numbers between 10 and 30 have a counter in the bin?

Which numbers between 10 and 30 do not have a counter in the bin?

What do you notice?

 sharing equally

The Language of Maths

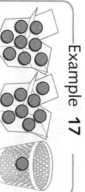

In division, we sometimes use the word 'remainder'.

What does this mean?

remainder

The Maths Herald

Name:

Date:

Looking for Patterns

Write an addition (+) or subtraction (–) sign in each diamond ◇ to make each number sentence true.

5 ◇ 2 ◇ 3 = 10   9 ◇ 3 ◇ 2 = 10

3 ◇ 2 ◇ 1 = 2   6 ◇ 3 ◇ 2 = 1

7 ◇ 5 ◇ 2 = 4   8 ◇ 2 ◇ 5 = 5

Money Matters

Using only 5p, 10p and 20p coins, how many different ways can you make 40p?

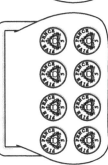

40p

Around the World

Lisa walks from her home to the shops.

As she walks add +2 or take away –2 the numbers.

What different totals can you make?

sum

+2

+1

−1

−2

−4

+1

−2

−3

+4

−2

+3

+5

−2

+2

+5

+2

−1

Lisa's home

−2

+5

+4

+3

+3

−3

The Puzzler

1, 2, 3, 4, 5, 6, 7, 8, 9, 10

The numbers 2 and 5 have a sum of 7 and a difference of 3.

Which 2 numbers above have:

- a sum of 6 and a difference of 2?
- a sum of 10 and a difference of 4?
- a sum of 9 and a difference of 7?
- a sum of 15 and a difference of 3?
- a sum of 15 and a difference of 5?

$2 + 5 = 7$

$5 - 2 = 3$

Let's Investigate

Using just the 3 numbers 2, 6 and 8 you can write these 4 number sentences:

$2 + 6 = 8$

$6 + 2 = 8$

$8 - 2 = 6$

$8 - 6 = 2$

What number sentences can you write from each of these sets of 3 numbers?

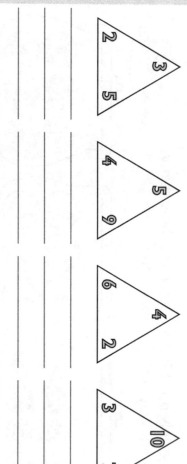

Let's Investigate

Can you think of 4 other sets of 3 numbers that each give 2 addition and 2 subtraction number sentences? What are the number sentences?

Look at the different sets of 3 numbers in the Let's Investigate activity on page 2.

The Puzzler

 + = 25p

+ + = 15p

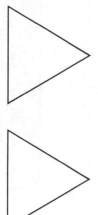 + = 70p

What is the cost of a ?

What is the cost of a ?

What is the cost of a ?

What is the cost of a  + ?

The Maths Herald

Name: _____

Date: _____

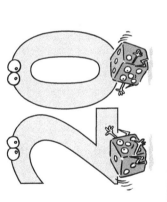

total [ ]

🐭 The Puzzler

Draw a path through the maze.

You must move from a number to a plus (+) or minus (–) sign and then to another number.

You can only move up or down ↕ or across ↔ (not diagonally ↘ ↙).

START →

3	+	2	+	5
+	+	3	–	+
4	–	–	–	2
–	+	2	3	+
2	+	5	–	4 = 4 END

🐭 The Puzzler

You need:
• 2 1–6 dice
• some counters

12	14	9	17	8
8	16	10	11	13
15	12	17	14	15
16	18	14	18	9
10	11	13	12	13

Take turns to:
• roll the 2 dice

• add the 2 numbers together and say the total

"4 and 5 is 9."

• subtract this number from 20 and say the answer

"20 subtract 9 is 11."

• place a counter on that number on the grid.

The winner is the first player to complete a line of 4 counters. The line can be along a row ↔ or a column ↕ or a diagonal ↘ ↗.

Looking for Patterns

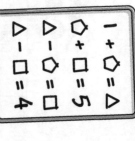

Each board is missing 3 different numbers: □, ◇ and △.
What are the numbers?

$$1 + □ = ◇$$
$$□ + □ = 5$$
$$△ - ◇ = □$$
$$△ - □ = 4$$

$$3 + □ = △$$
$$□ + ◇ = 10$$
$$△ - □ = ◇$$
$$△ - ◇ = 7$$

$$2 + ◇ = □$$
$$◇ + △ = □$$
$$□ - 6 = △$$
$$8 - △ = □$$

The Puzzler

A	B	C	D	E	F
8	6	5	10	7	3

Use the numbers above to work out the answers to these problems.

A + F = ☐

B – F = ☐

D + E = ☐

E – C = ☐   B + C + D = ☐

A – F = ☐   E + F – D = ☐

D shared between C is ☐   C lots of D is ☐

Money Matters

Use these coins to make each side add up to £2.

Use these coins to make each side add up to 80p.

Use these coins to make each side add up to £1.70.

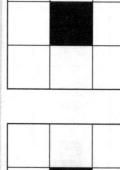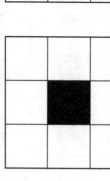

The Puzzler

Look at the 6 numbers in 🧩 The Puzzler on page 2.
Which letters give these answers?

☐ + ☐ = 16

☐ – ☐ = 4

☐ + ☐ = 20

☐ + ☐ = 12

lots of ☐ is 30

☐ shared between ☐ is 2

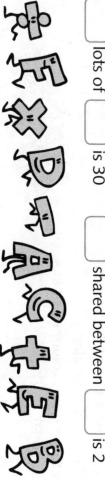

© HarperCollins Publishers 2016

S&C Volume 1

The Maths Herald

Name:

Date:

Technology Today

> Using only the 1, 2, 3 or 4 number keys, I can make answers of 5 and 3.

What other numbers can you make using only the 1, 2, 3 or 4 number keys?

Let's Investigate

Using 1, 2, 3 or 4 darts for each number, can you make all the numbers from 1 to 20?

Here are 2 to get you started.

$6 = 5 + 1$

$14 = 10 + 2 + 2$

Money Matters

Money goes into the moneybox and some of it falls out.

This moneybox has 70p left inside.

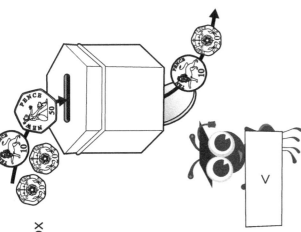

How much money does each of these moneyboxes have left inside?

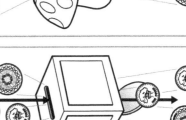

Money Matters

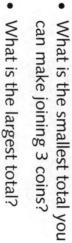

- Draw a line joining 3 coins.

  How much money is this?

- Draw another line joining 3 coins.

  How much money is this?

- Draw a third line joining 3 coins.

  How much money is this?

- What is the smallest total you can make joining 3 coins?

  How much money is this?

- What is the largest total?

Let's Investigate

Using only these numbers, how many different number sentences can you write with an answer of 10?

You can only use each number once in each number sentence.

Here are 3 to get you started.

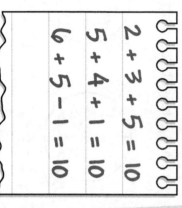

2 + 3 + 5 = 10

5 + 4 + 1 = 10

6 + 5 − 1 = 10

Looking for Patterns

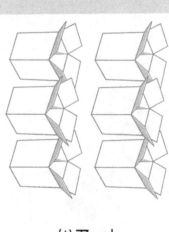

4 counters have been put into these 3 boxes. Each box must have at least 1 counter in it.

There are 2 other ways you can put the 4 counters into the 3 boxes. What are they?

There are 6 different ways of putting 5 counters into the 3 boxes. What are they?

The Maths Herald

Name:

Date:

Let's Investigate

Think of a number and write it on the engine – perhaps your favourite number.

In each carriage, write a number sentence that has as its answer the number on the engine.

Can you think of any more number sentences?

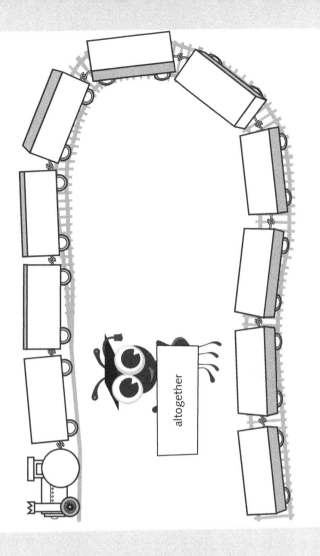

altogether

The Puzzler

Play this game with a friend.

You need:
- ten 1p coins
- five 2p coins
- five 10p coins

- Each player chooses a moneybox and writes their name in the box below it.

- Take turns to choose a 1p or 2p coin and put it on the hand.

- Count up the total on the hand as you go along.

- The player placing the coin that makes the amount on the hand exactly 10p exchanges the coins for a 10p piece and puts the 10p in their moneybox.

- The winner is the first player with 3 10p coins in their moneybox.

- Play the game several times.

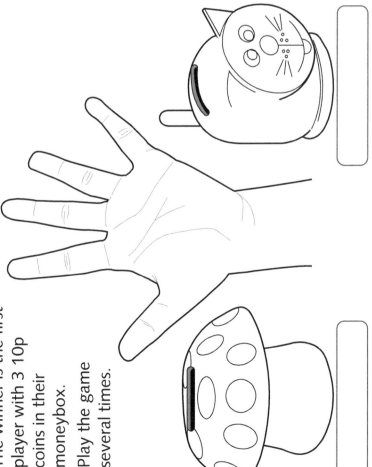

Money Matters

Investigate other amounts of money you can make using only 3 of these coins.

Using only 3 of these coins I can make 65p.

Let's Investigate

Using these cards, you can make these number sentences with an answer of 5.

```
0  1  2  3  4
5  6  7  8  9
+  -  =
```

This number sentence uses 5 cards.

```
4  +  1  =  5
```

This number sentence uses 6 cards.

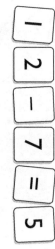
```
1  2  -  7  =  5
```

This number sentence uses 7 cards.

```
2  3  -  1  8  =  5
```

What other number sentences with an answer of 5 can you make using 5, 6 or 7 cards?

You can only use each card once in a number sentence.

2

Money Matters

What is the total value of this line of coins?

☐

Now replace every 2nd coin with a 20p coin. What is the total value of the line now?

For each line of coins, work out the total value before and after coins are replaced.

Before:    After: ☐

Replace every 2nd coin with a 1p coin.

Before: ☐   After: ☐

Replace every 2nd coin with a 50p coin.

Before: ☐   After: ☐

Replace every 3rd coin with a 2p coin.

Before: After: ☐

Replace every 2nd coin with a 10p coin.

3

The Maths Herald

S&C Volume 1

Name:

Date:

Money Matters

Ruby and Susan opened their moneyboxes.

Susan had £7 in her moneybox. What coins might Susan have had in her moneybox?

The rest of the money on the table was in Ruby's moneybox.

How much money was in Ruby's moneybox?

What coins might Ruby have had in her moneybox?

Looking for Patterns

Cut out the pictures of dogs, cats and chickens.

Here is one group of 12 animals made from 2 different animals.

What other groups of 12 animals can you make using 2 different animals?

Now make some groups of 12 animals using all 3 animals. Write a number sentence for each group.

Looking for Patterns

Take 4 counters. Put 1 counter in each box. How many counters is this altogether?

	BOX 1	BOX 2	BOX 3	BOX 4	Total number of counters
4 counters	1	1	1	1	4
+ 4 more	2	2	2	2	8
+ 4 more					
+ 4 more					
+ 4 more					

Take 4 more counters and put 1 counter in each box. How many counters is this altogether?

Now take 4 more counters.

Put 1 in each box.

In the table, write down how many counters are now in each box.

How many counters is this altogether?

Keep taking 4 more counters until you complete the table.

Let's Investigate

Enter the house.

As you move from room to room you collect gold coins or lose gold coins.

Leave the house through the Exit.

How many different ways can you move through the house?

How many gold coins do you end up with each time?

Rule

On each journey through the house you can only go into each room once.

Exit

Collect **5** gold coins

Lose **3** gold coins

Lose **4** gold coins

Collect **3** gold coins

Collect **4** gold coins

Lose **5** gold coins

Collect **6** gold coins

Lose **2** gold coins

Lose **1** gold coin

Collect **10** gold coins

Enter

Looking for Patterns

Harvey rolled 6 dice.

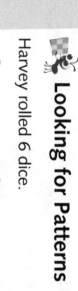

He then moved the dice to this order because it made it easier for him to add up the dice.

Why did Harvey think this was easier?

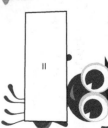

$=$

Looking for Patterns

You need 6 1–6 dice.

Roll the dice and write down the numbers rolled.

Just like Harvey in the 🐜 Looking for Patterns activity above, move the dice to make them easier to add.

Why is this easier?

The Maths Herald

Name:

Date:

What's the Problem?

cost

What is the cost of 4 cones?

What is the cost of 1 cone?

What is the cost of 3 cones?

Sports Update

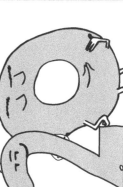

Roshan plays for her local football team.

Her number is less than 63 but greater than 11.

If you add 37 to her number, you get 61.

Her number is 18 less than 42.

Take away 15 from her number and you get 9.

What number is Roshan?

Let's Investigate

$6 + 4 = 10$

$3 + 5 + 2 = 10$

$14 - 4 = 10$

All these number sentences make 10.

Write some more number sentences that make 10.

Look at your list of number sentences that make 10.

Use this to help you write some number sentences that make 20.

$16 + 4 = 20$

$6 + 10 + 4 = 20$

$24 - 4 = 20$

The Puzzler

Draw 1 ring around 3 numbers that total 16.

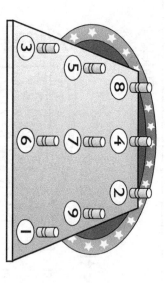

Draw another ring around 3 numbers that total 21.

Technology Today

Work out what number went into each machine.

IN [ ] +2 → OUT 6

IN [ ] -3 → OUT 5

IN [ ] double → OUT 8

IN [ ] +5 → OUT 9

IN [ ] halve → OUT 6

IN [ ] -8 → OUT 2

Looking for Patterns

Cut out the pictures of dogs, cats and chickens from the sheet.

Here is one way you can make a group of animals with 6 ears altogether.

How many ways can you make a group with 6 ears?

Here is a group with 10 legs altogether.

How many ways can you make a group with 10 legs?

Let's Investigate

Using only these numbers and signs, I can make 8 different number sentences and their answers.

3 + 2 = 5

| 2 | 3 | 5 | 8 |

| + | – | = |

Is Kate right?

S&C Volume 1

The Maths Herald

Name:

Date:

The Puzzler

Divide this cake into 4 equal pieces with 2 straight cuts.

Now make 8 equal pieces with 2 more cuts.

Use a different coloured pencil.

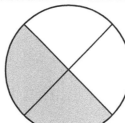

Happy ✶ Birthday

$\frac{1}{2}$

Let's Investigate

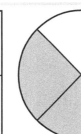

Half of this square is shaded.

Half of this circle is shaded.

Use the sheet to show other ways to shade half of the square and the circle.

Focus on Science

Circle $\frac{1}{2}$ of the bees.

Circle $\frac{1}{2}$ of the flies.

Circle $\frac{1}{4}$ of the spiders.

Circle $\frac{1}{2}$ of the worms.

Circle $\frac{1}{4}$ of the beetles.

Circle $\frac{1}{4}$ of the ladybirds.

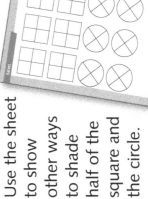

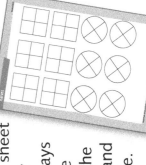

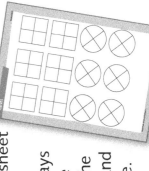

Looking for Patterns

3 squares are cut in half and shaded in these three ways.

4 halves can be put together to make these two different squares.

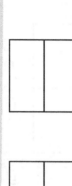

Shade these squares so that they are all different.

What's the Problem?

What fraction of these are fish?

Draw in more fish so that $\frac{1}{4}$ of all are crabs.

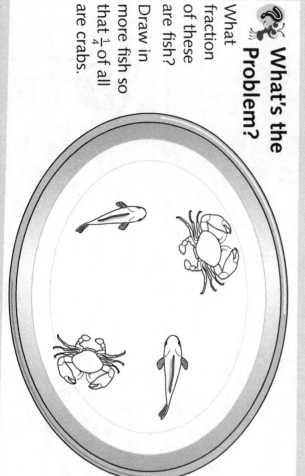

Let's Investigate

Colour half of each of these shapes.

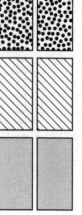
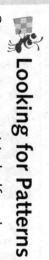

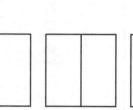
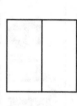

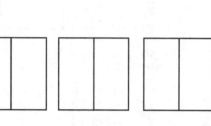

The Puzzler

Kath and Kim eat a small Strawberry Log between them.

Kath makes one cut to divide the log in half.

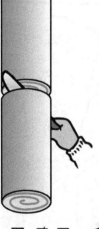

5 friends eat a large Strawberry Log between them.

How many cuts are needed to divide the log into five pieces?

The Maths Herald

Name:

Date:

The Arts Roundup

Colour $\frac{1}{2}$ of the dresses yellow.

Now draw a crown on $\frac{1}{4}$ of the heads.

Construct

Fold a sheet of paper in half.

Fold it in half again.

Open it out and write $\frac{1}{4}$ in each quarter.

$\frac{1}{4}$	$\frac{1}{4}$
$\frac{1}{4}$	$\frac{1}{4}$

Investigate different ways of folding a sheet of paper into quarters.

Money Matters

Draw lines to match coins with the same value.

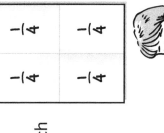

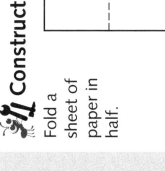

Half of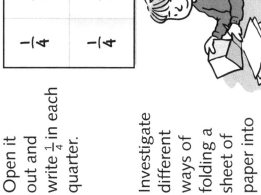

Half of

Half of

Half of

Half of

Half of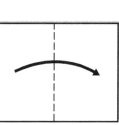

Let's Investigate

A quarter of this rectangle is shaded.

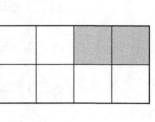

A quarter of this circle is shaded.

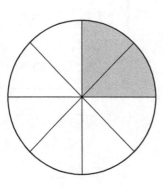

Use the sheet to show other ways to shade a quarter of the rectangle and the circle.

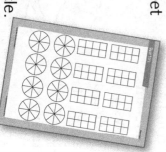

Let's Investigate

Each of these shapes is half of another shape.

Investigate what the whole shapes might look like.

$\frac{1}{4}$

The Puzzler

Wilber used interlocking cubes to make a rod 4 cubes long:

- How many cubes would Wilber need to make a rod half the length of his rod?

- How many cubes would Wilber need to make a rod a quarter of the length of his rod?

Wilber then made a second rod. This rod is half the size of Wilber's second rod.

This rod is a quarter the size of Wilber's second rod.

- How many cubes did Wilber use to build his second rod?

The Puzzler

Work with a friend.

Take a sheet of paper and fold it in half to make a tunnel like this:

Each of you secretly makes a train. Use 4, 8, or 12 cubes to make your train.

Secretly place your train of cubes inside the tunnel so that only half or a quarter of your train is showing.

Tell your partner what fraction of your train is showing.

Can your partner guess how many cubes long your train is?

The Maths Herald

Name:

Date:

3 is a quarter of 12.

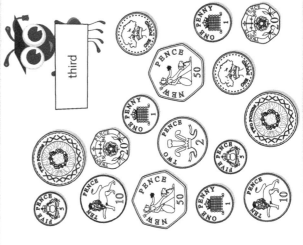

third

🐝 Let's Investigate

Is Gina right?

Find other pairs of numbers where one number is a quarter of the other.

What do you notice about the pairs of numbers?

💷 Money Matters

is half of

Find other pairs of coins where one coin is half the other coin.

Can you find a pair of coins where one coin is a quarter of the other coin?

🐜 The Language of Maths

Play this game with a friend.

Take turns to:

- roll the dice, e.g. 4
- find a statement on the board that is the answer to the number rolled, e.g. $\frac{1}{2}$ of 8
- say the statement to your partner
- put a counter on that statement on the board.

If you can't go, miss a turn.

Half of 8 is 4.

You need:
- 12 counters
- 1–6 dice

The winner is the first player to complete a line of 3 counters.

$\frac{1}{2}$ of 8	$\frac{1}{2}$ of 2	Quarter of 20	Half of 6
Quarter of 4	$\frac{1}{4}$ of 24	Half of 10	$\frac{1}{4}$ of 8
$\frac{1}{4}$ of 12	Half of 4	Quarter of 16	$\frac{1}{2}$ of 12

The Puzzler

Jack ate $\frac{1}{2}$ of his cherries and had 7 left.

How many cherries did he start with?

How many cherries did Jack eat?

Jill ate $\frac{1}{2}$ of her cherries and had 6 left.

How many cherries did she start with?

How many cherries did Jill eat?

What's the Problem?

How many bees are there?

$\frac{1}{2}$ fly away.

How many are left?

What if $\frac{1}{4}$ flew away instead?

How many would be left?

The Puzzler

Lee cut her pizza into 4 slices. She then ate 2 of these slices.

Divide Lee's pizza into 4 equal pieces and colour 2 of the pieces.

Amy cut her pizza into 8 slices. She then ate 3 of these slices.

Divide Amy's pizza into 8 equal pieces and colour 3 of the pieces.

Who ate more pizza, Lee or Amy?

Money Matters

How much money does Jake have altogether?

$\frac{1}{2}$ of all the money I have is £3.

How much money does Ceri have altogether?

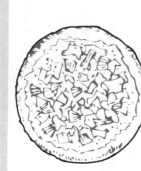

$\frac{1}{4}$ of all the money I have is £2.

S&C Volume 1

The Maths Herald

Name:

Date:

Let's Investigate

Use string
to measure
the sides
of each of
these shapes.

distance

The Puzzler

Charlotte used interlocking cubes
to make a tower 5 cubes high:

- How many cubes would Charlotte
  need to make a tower twice as high?

- How many cubes would Charlotte
  need to make a tower 3 times as high?

Charlotte then made a
second tower.

This tower is twice the height of
Charlotte's second tower.

This tower is 4 times the height of
Charlotte's second tower.

- How many cubes did Charlotte
  use to build her second tower?

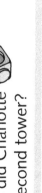

At Home

You need:
- some toys
- string or wool
- ruler

Choose some toys that are all different in size.

Take one of the toys and, using the piece of string,
measure how tall and how wide it is.

Place the piece of string against
the ruler to find out how many
centimetres tall and wide it is.

Write down the name of the toy
and its measurements.

Do the same for the other toys.

4

🌍 Around the World

- Which bear takes the most footsteps to the honey pot?
  How many steps is this?
- Which bear takes the least footsteps to the honey pot?
  How many steps is this?

🏠 At Home

How many steps does it take to walk from the front door of your home to the nearest shop?

You don't need to give the exact number. Talk to an adult at home about what the answer might be.

Do you think that you would take the same number of steps as an adult? Why do you think this?

🔬 Focus on Science

Which do you think is longer – your handspan or the distance around your wrist?

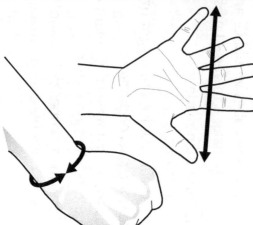

Write down which you think is longer.

Now find out.

Was your prediction correct?

Do you think this will be the same for other children in your class?

Find out.

The Maths Herald

Name:

Date:

Looking for Patterns

2 stars ☆ weigh the same as 1 cross ✚

3 stars ☆ weigh the same as 1 heart ♥

Draw stars ☆ so that each scale balances.

Draw crosses ✚ and hearts ♥ so that each scale balances.

Let's Investigate

What do you think is the lightest object in your classroom?

What do you think is the heaviest object in your classroom?

Write about why you think your objects are the lightest and the heaviest.

Let's Investigate

You need:

- balance
- spoon
- rice
- 0–9 dice
- 1 kg weight

Play this game with a friend.

Before you start place the 1 kg weight on the balance.

Take turns to:

- roll the dice
- collect that many spoonfuls of rice
- put the rice on the balance.

The winner is the player whose spoonful makes more than 1 kg of rice.

What if you tried this game with pasta or sugar or flour? Would the game take as long? Might it be quicker? Might it take longer?

Why?

Play another game using something other than rice to find out.

At Home

Take a cup and fill it with something.

It might be something that you use to cook with, like sugar, flour, raisins or rice.

It might be something else like paper clips, buttons or pebbles.

Weigh the cup. Write down what it weighs.

Now empty the cup and fill it with something else.

Do you think the cup will weigh the same, weigh more or weigh less?

Weigh the cup and find out.

Do this a few more times.

Write about what you find out.

Focus on Science

The weight of something heavy is measured in **kilograms** (kg).

The weight of something light is measured in **grams** (g).

One interlocking cube weighs 4 grams.

What is the weight of each of these shapes?

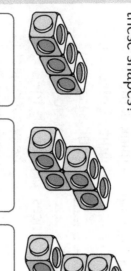
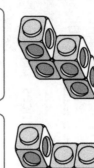
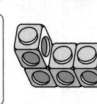
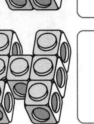
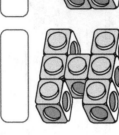

Let's Investigate

Choose five objects in your classroom that you can lift easily.

Place them in a line from heaviest to lightest. Write down your results.

Now use a scale balance to see if you are right.

Were you right?

Which objects were hardest to place in order? Why was this?

Looking for Patterns

Work out the value of the third balance in each of these puzzles.

If ● 5 and ✚ 2 then ●✚ 7

If ◆ ▷ 1 and ◎ ▷ 6 then ◎◆ ▷

If ✚ ▷ 3 and ✦ ▷ 4 then ✚✚✦ ▷

If ○○ ▷ 10 and ○ ▷ 7 then ○○ ▷

Let's Investigate

You need:
- book
- set of measuring scales

What is the weight of the book?

What do you think will be the weight of 10 books?

Now weigh 10 books to find out.

Were you right?

Choose another object and weigh it. Estimate what 10 of the objects will weigh then check to see if you are right.

Write about what you discover.

balance

The Maths Herald

Name:

Date:

Let's Investigate

Make a list of all the things you could fit inside a matchbox.

gallon

Let's Investigate

An activity to do with a friend.

How much water can you each hold in your hands?

Here's what to do:

- Take turns to make a 'cup' using both your hands.
- Hold your hands under the tap while your friend slowly turns on the tap.
- When your hands are full of water, carefully tip the water into the bowl.
- Then carefully pour the water from the bowl into the measuring jug.

You need:

- tap
- bowl
- 1 litre measuring jug

© HarperCollins Publishers 2016

Focus on Science

An activity to do with a friend.

Fill each of the containers with one type of object such as marbles.

Do not count the marbles as you put them in each container.

Take one of the containers and each guess how many marbles it holds.

Write down what each of you thinks.

Now count the marbles in the container.

Write down how many marbles there are.

Do the same for all the other containers.

When you have guessed and counted how many marbles there are in each container, fill each of the containers with another type of object such as cubes. Do the activity again.

Do the activity several times for the other small objects.

You need:

- some small containers such as yoghurt pot, paper cup, egg cup and paint pot
- a lot of different small objects such as cubes, marbles, paper clips or pasta shells

Container	Ryan's guess	Leroy's guess	Number of objects
yoghurt pot	30	35	28 marbles
paper cup			

The Language of Maths

litre and pint

Some people use the word 'litres' to talk about how much a container holds.

Other people use the word 'pints'.

What is the difference between a litre and a pint?

Let's Investigate

Whose handful has the greatest capacity?

Who in your class can hold the most in their hand?

Choose something small that you have a lot of in the classroom. It might be cubes, marbles, paper clips or pasta shells.

Ask everyone to take a handful of your chosen object.

Count how many each person can hold.

Draw a table to keep a record of your results.

Write about what you find out.

You need:

- some small objects that you have a lot of such as cubes, marbles, paper clips or pasta shells

Name	Number of cubes

Let's Investigate

How many cups do you think the bottle holds?

Now check by carefully pouring the water into the cups.

How close was your guess?

You need:

- large bottle of mineral water
- some paper cups

Focus on Science

An activity to do with a friend.

You need:

- some small containers such as yoghurt pot, paper cup, egg cup and paint pot
- 1 litre measuring jug
- water

Take one of the small containers, such as a yoghurt pot, and fill it with water.

Both of you point to where you think one potful of water would come to on the measuring jug.

Now pour the water from the pot into the measuring jug.

How close were your guesses?

Empty the jug. Do the same for the other small containers.

At Home

Look around the home for lots of different containers.

Write down your order.

Now, with the help of an adult, read the labels on each of the containers and once more put the containers in order starting with the container that holds the least.

Write down your order.

Are the 2 orders the same?

Without looking at the labels, put the containers in order starting with the container that holds the least.

The Maths Herald

Name:

Date:

The Language of Maths

Choose 5 different times during the day.

Show these times on the clocks.

Write about what you are doing at each of these times.

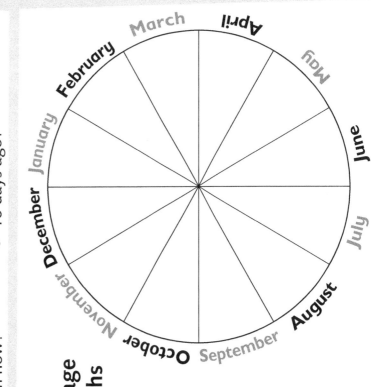

At Home

Talk to someone at home about what they do at different times during the day.

Show this on the sheet.

Ask 2 other people – maybe a brother or sister, or perhaps even a neighbour.

© HarperCollins Publishers 2016

What's the Problem?

Imagine that today is Sunday.

Flower Garden
OPEN
This Sunday
TODAY

What day of the week will it be:

- 4 days from now?
- 9 days from now?
- 12 days from now?
- 16 days from now?

What day of the week was it:

- 4 days ago?
- 9 days ago?
- 12 days ago?
- 16 days ago?

The Language of Maths

Write or draw something that happens for each month of the year.

January
February
March
April
May
June
July
August
September
October
November
December

What's the Problem?

Lucy was 8 years old in 2015.

How old was she in 2010?

How old will she be in 2024?

The Language of Maths

Look at the clock on the right.

What is the time:

- 2 hours after this time?
- 5 hours after this time?
- $3\frac{1}{2}$ hours after this time?
- 6 hours before this time?
- $4\frac{1}{2}$ hours before this time?

annual

The Language of Maths

A calendar is a chart that shows the months of the year and the days of the week.

This calendar is for the month of September.

September						
S	M	T	W	T	F	S
		1	2	3	4	5
6	7	8	9	10	11	12
13	14	15	16	17	18	19
20	21	22	23	24	25	26
27	28	29	30			

Work with a partner.

Take turns to ask each other questions about the calendar.

Here are 2 to get you started.

What day is the 29th September?

How many Mondays in September?

Let's Investigate

Make a list of things that take about 1 minute or less.

How many of each of the following things can you do in 1 minute?

- Use a stopwatch or the seconds hand on a clock to time yourself.
- Write your name.
- Tie and untie your shoe laces.
- Walk around your table.
- Build towers of 5 interlocking cubes.

S&C Volume 1

The Maths Herald

Name:

Date:

🏠 At Home

About how far do you travel to and from school in a week?

What about any brothers and sisters you might have?

If there is someone at home who works, how far do they travel to and from work in a week?

Over a week, you and the members of your family travel to other places, such as the supermarket, to visit friends or to a club after school or work. Apart from school and work, how far do you and the other members of your family travel each week?

🧪 Focus on Science

An activity to do with a friend.

Make ice cubes using different types of liquid.

You might have an ice cube made from:

- water
- water and salt
- water and sugar
- fruit juice
- fizzy drink

What else can you think of to make ice cubes from?

Put the ice cube tray in the freezer and wait for the liquids to freeze.

Then take the ice cubes out and place them on a plate.

Which ice cube melts the quickest?

Which ice cube melts the slowest?

Write about what you find out.

> **You need:**
> - ice cube tray
> - water, salt, sugar, fruit juice, fizzy drink

Let's Investigate

Choose 2 containers in the classroom where you think that one container holds about half the capacity of the other container.

Then work out a way to see if you were right.

Looking for Patterns

This scale balances:

So does this scale:

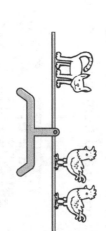

Use the dogs, cats and chickens at the bottom of the sheet to balance the 4 scales at the top of the sheet.

time-line

At Home

Make a time-line for your family.

Draw a long line. Start by writing the years that your parents, or even your grandparents, were born.

On the time-line write all the important things that have happened to your family. Make sure to mark on your time-line the year, and if you know it, even the date.

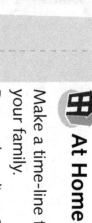

1952   1955   1956

Grandpa Nanna Ann &   Nanna
Tom born Grandpa Jim   Mary
          born   born

Let's Investigate

We measure things when we want to find out how long or how heavy they are.

We also measure things to find out how much something holds or what time it is.

Look around the classroom. What things can you find that are used to measure something?

Record your results in a table.

Object	Used to measure
clock	time

The Maths Herald

Name:

Date:

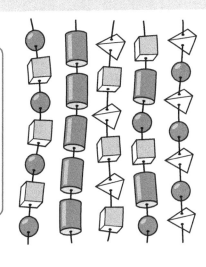

You need:
- wooden beads
- lace or string
- interlocking cubes
- measuring scales

Construct

Use the beads to make a necklace as near to 200 grams as you can.

How many beads did you use to make your necklace?

If you made another necklace as near to 200 grams that used interlocking cubes instead of wooden beads, would you use more or fewer cubes?

Explain why.

Now use cubes to find out if what you thought was right.

gram

At Home

Chinese years are organised by animals.

2013 was the Year of the Snake.

2014 was the Year of the Horse.

2015 was the Year of the Sheep.

Ask your family and friends to tell you in which year they were born.

Then use the Chinese Calendar to work out which Chinese year this was.

Write what you find out in the table.

Name	Year of birth	Chinese year

The Language of Maths

Look around the classroom.

Find something **lighter** than your chair, but **heavier** than your shoe.

Find something taller than you, but shorter than your teacher.

Find something longer than a pencil, but shorter than a ruler.

The Language of Maths

Find a paintbrush.
Look for objects in the classroom to compare with the paintbrush.

A little shorter	
A lot shorter	
About the same	
A little longer	
A lot longer	

Find a chair.
Look for objects in the classroom to compare with the chair.

A little lighter	
A lot lighter	
About the same	
A little **heavier**	
A lot **heavier**	

Focus on Science

An activity to do with a friend.

Take a sponge and soak it in water.

Then squeeze all the water out of the sponge and into a large bowl.

Carefully pour the water from the bowl into the measuring jug.

How much water does the sponge hold?

Do the same for all the other sponges.

What did you find out?

You need:
- water
- some different sponges
- large bowl
- measuring jug

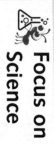

Money Matters

Is money a measure?
Explain why.

S&C Volume 1

The Maths Herald

Name:

Date:

🐜 In the Past

These puzzles are from Ancient Greece.

Cut out the first cross on the sheet and cut it up along the lines.

Put the 4 pieces together to make a square.

Cut out the second cross and cut it up along the lines.

Put the 4 pieces together to make another square.

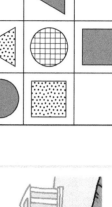

🧩 The Puzzler

Draw the shapes to complete each of the grids.

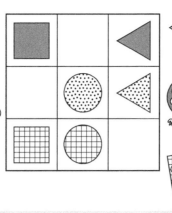

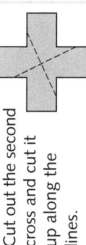

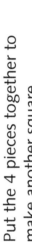

🐜 Let's Investigate

Look at this pattern of triangles.

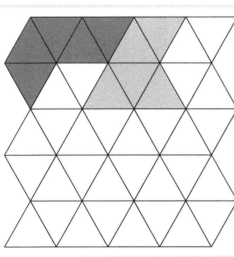

Each of these two shapes has been made by colouring 5 triangles.

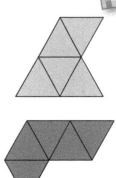

Using the first grid on the sheet, what other shapes can you make by colouring 5 triangles?

🐜 Construct

Look at the different shapes you made in the 🐜 Let's Investigate activity opposite.

Can you use these different shapes so that every triangle on this pattern of triangles is coloured?

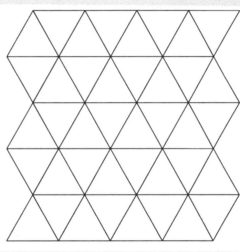

Use the second grid on the sheet to show your pattern.

value

Looking for Patterns

Altogether
there are
8 triangles
in this
diagram.

On each of these diagrams
colour a different triangle.

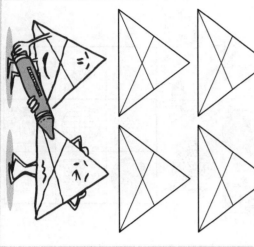

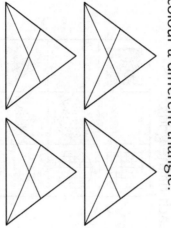

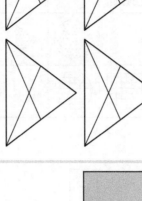

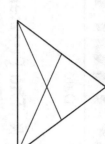

Let's Investigate

Cut out the
4 shapes on
the sheet.

Put 2 shapes
together, side
by side, to
make another.

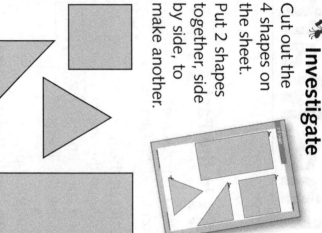

Draw your shape.

How many different shapes
can you make?

What if you put 3 shapes
together?

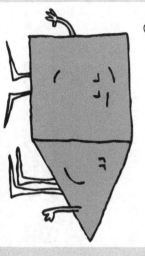

Let's Investigate

In each diagram, join up the dots with
straight lines to make the shapes.

All the shapes must be the same size. Use all the dots.

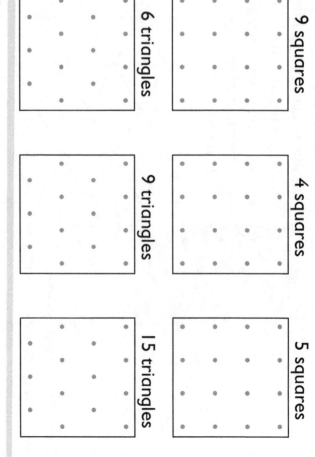

9 squares

4 squares

5 squares

6 triangles

9 triangles

15 triangles

The Puzzler

Look at the value of
each of these shapes.

Write the values on each part of these shapes.

| 2 | 1 | 3 | | 5 |

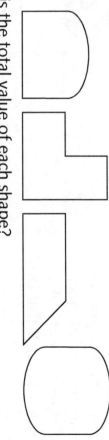

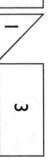

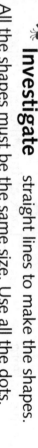

What is the total value of each shape?

S&C Volume 1

The Maths Herald

Name:

Date:

🐜 Construct

Using the sheet, cut out the house along the – – – – – – – lines.

Fold the house together along the .... lines.

Now open up your house and draw on windows and doors.

Now use the tabs to glue your house together.

🐞 Let's Investigate

Work with a friend.

Find an empty box.

Carefully cut the box in half so that both halves are the same.

🕷 Looking for Patterns

I

2

3

4

Each of the shapes above has been moved into different positions and drawn below.

Label each of the shapes below along with the matching number.

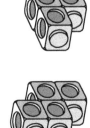

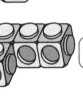

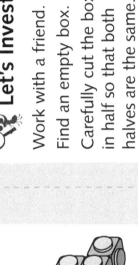

Let's Investigate

You can make this shape using 4 cubes.

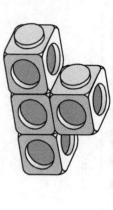

Can you make them all?

It is possible to make another 7 different shapes using 4 cubes.

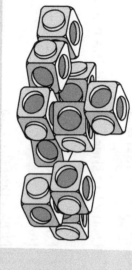

At Home

Play 'Hunt the 3-D shape'. Find an adult. Take them into the kitchen and open up all the cupboards!

Secretly choose an object. The adult asks questions to try and find out which object you have chosen.

Good questions might be:

> Does it have 6 faces?

> Does the object have a round face?

> Is it the same shape as a cereal box?

> Is it larger or smaller than a tin of soup?

Play the game several times, changing roles.

Construct

Look at this house.

Can you make the same shape using different shaped solid blocks?

Draw your house shape, showing the blocks.

Can you make a bigger house shape?

Draw this shape too.

The Language of Maths

cube	square-based pyramid	triangular-based pyramid
	cuboid	

Draw lines from each 3-D shape to the 2-D shapes that show the different faces of each 3-D shape. Some 3-D shapes may be joined to more than one 2-D shape.

3-D

The Maths Herald

Name:

Date:

 **Let's Investigate**

Each of these shapes are symmetrical.
They each have 8 squares coloured.

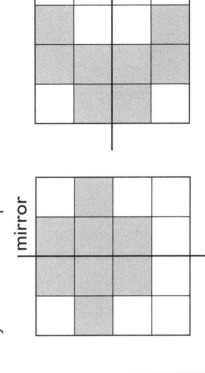

mirror

mirror

symmetrical

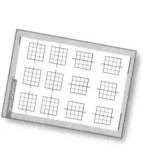

Using the sheet, show different symmetrical patterns by colouring 8 squares on each grid.

Construct

All these shapes have symmetry.
Draw the missing half of each shape.

🐜 Construct

Colour the rug so that it makes a pattern.
Use only 4 colours.

🏁🐜 Looking for Patterns

You can make 8 different towers using only blue and red blocks.

Here are 3.

Colour these blocks to show the other 6.

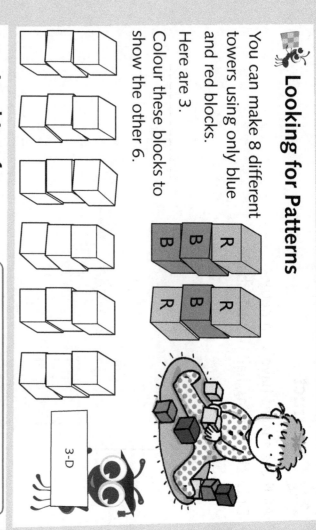

3-D

🏁🐜 Looking for Patterns

Play this game with a friend. Use the sheet.

You need:
- 32 counters all the same colour

- One player puts 1, 2 or 3 counters on the grey dots.

- The other player then puts counters on the white dots to make a symmetrical pattern.

- Keep going until all the dots have a counter on them and you have made a symmetrical pattern.

- Repeat, swapping roles.

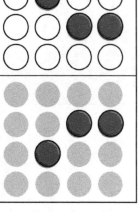

© HarperCollinsPublishers 2016

S&C Volume 1

The Maths Herald

Name:

Date:

🏠 At Home

Find an interesting piece of furniture.

Draw three pictures of the furniture.

- View from the front
- View from the side
- View from above looking down

The Puzzler

Jean, Lee, Sundus, Aimee and Amanda are all sitting at a round table.

Amanda is between Lee and Sundus.

Sundus is sitting on Jean's right and Aimee is sitting on Lee's right.

Label the diagram to show where each girl is sitting.

🐜 Construct

Your headteacher wants a set of maps showing the way from the school office to each classroom.

These can then be given to visitors to help them find their way around the school.

Draw the map from the school office to your classroom.

Make sure you label your map.

The Language of Maths

Ollie is standing in a line.

He is 2nd from the front of the line and 6th from the back of the line.

There are 7 children standing in the line.

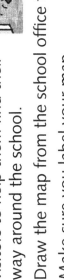

map

Hi! I'm Ollie

How many children are there in each of these lines?

- Ollie is 4th from the front and 3rd from the back.
- Ollie is 5th from the front and 5th from the back.
- Ollie is 3rd from the front and 5th from the back.

The Language of Maths

Cut out the 12 toys at the bottom of the sheet.

Follow the instructions and put the toys on the shelves.

The 🪀 goes **above** the 🥁 .

The 🚗 goes **above** the 🔨 .

The 🚙 goes to the **right** of the 🚗 .

The 🚗 goes to the **right** of the 🧸 .

The 🏉 goes **above** the 🐻 .

The 🏓 goes **above** the 🚗 .

The 🏐 goes to the **left** of the 🖍 .

The 🐻 goes to the **right** of the 🐻 .

The 🚗 goes **below** the 🏉 .

The 🚗 goes to the **right** of the 🚙 .

The 🕹 goes to the **right** of the 🚗 .

The 🎮 goes to the **left** of the 🚗 .

The 🍔 goes to the **left** of the 🏎 .

The 🚙 goes **above** the 🚗 .

The 🚗 goes **below** the 🏎 .

The Language of Maths

Cut out the 12 toys at the bottom of the sheet.

Find a friend.

One of you puts your toys in your cupboard without letting your friend see where you have put them.

Now describe to your friend where your toys are.

Your friend must follow your instructions and place their toys in the same places in their cupboard.

When they have placed all their toys, look at each other's cupboards. Do they look the same?

Now let your friend place their toys and describe where they are to you.

Construct

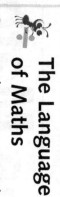

Tessellations are tiling patterns made by repeating one or more shapes so that they fit together without leaving gaps or overlapping.

Continue each of these patterns.

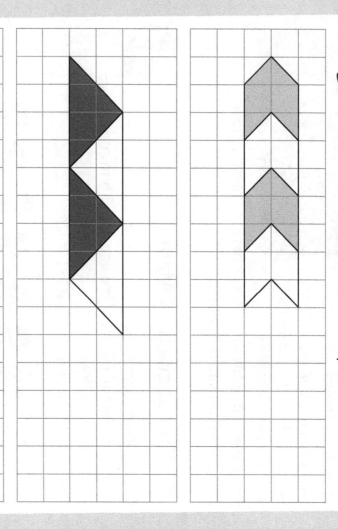

S&C Volume 1

The Maths Herald

Name:

Date:

clockwise

windows

tables

mat

door

🎵 The Language of Maths

Imagine you are standing in the middle of this classroom.

What will you be facing if you:

- Are facing the **tables** and turn clockwise a quarter turn ↷.

- Are facing the **windows** and turn clockwise a half turn ↷.

- Are facing the **door** and turn anti-clockwise a quarter turn ↶.

- Are facing the **mat** and turn clockwise a quarter turn ↷.

- Are facing the **windows** and turn clockwise a three-quarters turn ↷.

The Puzzler

Play this game with a friend.

You need:

- small Compare Bear
- coin
- pile of counters
- 1–6 dice

Take 0 counters

Take 3 counters

Take 1 counter

Take 2 counters

Before you start:

- place the Compare Bear on the star ☆ facing 'Take 0 counters'

- place the coin on 'Start'.

Take turns to:

- roll the dice and move the coin that number of spaces

- turn the Compare Bear as shown

- collect the number of counters as shown.

Keep going until the coin reaches the end. Count your counters. The winner is the player with more counters.

START

Quarter turn left · Quarter turn right · Quarter turn left · Half turn · Quarter turn right · Quarter turn left

Quarter turn right · Quarter turn left · Quarter turn right · Quarter turn left · Half turn · Quarter turn right

Quarter turn right · Quarter turn left · Half turn · Quarter turn right · Quarter turn left · Half turn

Half turn · Quarter turn right · Quarter turn left · Half turn · Quarter turn right · Quarter turn left

Quarter turn left · Quarter turn right · Half turn · Quarter turn right · Quarter turn left · Half turn

END

Looking for Patterns

Draw the next 3 shapes in each pattern.

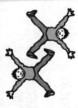

The Language of Maths

Follow the instructions and write down the numbers you land on. One has been done for you.

Put a counter on 'Start'.

Move **up** 2 spaces. → `23`

Move **up** 4 spaces.

Move to the **right** 3 spaces.

Move **up** 4 spaces.

Move to the **left** 2 spaces.

Move **down** 4 spaces.

Move to the **right** 3 spaces.

Move **up** 2 spaces.

Move to the **left** 1 space.

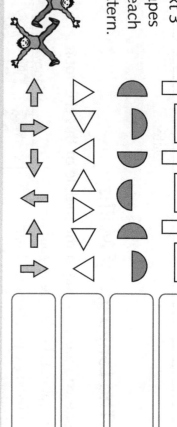

18	7	16	3	25	11
24	14	35	12	6	34
2	29	22	20	9	19
8	32	1	30	28	0
23	17	27	33	15	4
5	21	13	10	26	31

Start

The Language of Maths

Look at the grid in the activity on page 2.

Write the moves and the number of spaces you need to make to land on the numbers shown.

Begin at Start

Use words such as:

- up
- down
- to the right
- to the left

Move _____ spaces `23`

Move _____ spaces `19`

Move _____ spaces `4`

Move _____ spaces `27`

Move _____ spaces `35`

Move _____ spaces `14`

Move _____ spaces `21`

Move _____ spaces `31`

Looking for Patterns

Draw each of these shapes after they have been turned through half a turn.

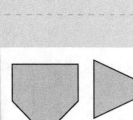

The Maths Herald

Name:

Date:

The Puzzler

Draw a shape in each box so that each row ↔ and column ↕ has one of each shape.

Looking for Patterns

How many triangles can you see?

quadrilateral

The Puzzler

Cut out the 5 shapes on the sheet.

You should now have 2 sets of these shapes – this set and the set from the Looking for Patterns activity on page 3.

Find a friend. You should now have 4 sets of these shapes.

Take the 4 shapes that look like this:

Arrange the 4 shapes to fit on the grid.

Show how you did it on squared paper.

Do the same using 4 of each of the other 4 shapes.

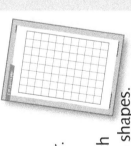

4 of the 5 different shapes will fit on the grid exactly. One will not fit. Which shape is this?

Looking for Patterns

Draw the next 3 shapes in each pattern.

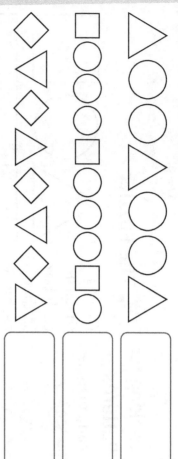

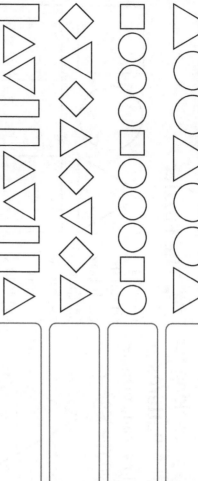

The Language of Maths

Find a friend and sit back to back.

Using a pile of different shapes, make a picture.

Describe your picture to your friend.

Can your friend make your picture?

Repeat, swapping roles.

Looking for Patterns

Cut out the 5 shapes on the sheet.

Put together 2, 3 or 4 of the shapes to make these shapes.

On squared paper show how you made these shapes.

1

2

3

4

5

6

Looking for Patterns

For each pattern, work out the rule then complete the last shape.

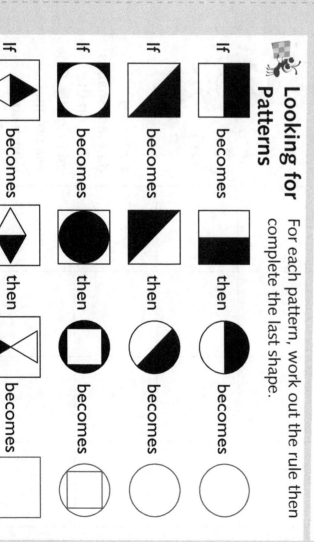

If   becomes   then   becomes

If   becomes   then   becomes

If   becomes   then   becomes

If   becomes   then   becomes

The Maths Herald

Name:

Date:

Construct

Origami is the Japanese art of paper folding.

Follow these instructions to make a boat.

You will need a sheet of coloured square paper.

Step 1. Fold the paper in half.

Step 2. Fold in half again.

Step 3. Fold the top layer down.

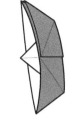

Step 4. Fold the other three flaps back and press hard.

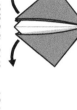

Step 5. Your paper should now look like this.

Step 6. Put your thumbs inside and open out the model. Press it down to make a square.

Step 7. Gently pull the flaps and flatten to make the boat.

Your boat should look like this.

Let's Investigate

Use a geoboard and elastic band to make some shapes. What shapes can you make that have just 1 pin in the centre?

What shapes can you make that have 2 pins in the centre?

Can you make some shapes that have no pins in the centre?

Draw your shapes on squared dot paper.

Let's Investigate

Use a geoboard and elastic band to make some triangles. What triangles can you make that have just 1 pin in the centre?

What triangles can you make that have 2 pins in the centre?

What about triangles with 3, 4, 5,… pins in the centres.

Can you make some triangles that have no pins in the centre?

Draw your triangles on squared dot paper.

polygon

The Puzzler

Jo dropped some tiles.
Before he dropped these tiles there were 8 of them.

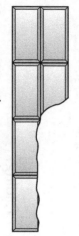

How many tiles were in each of these sets before Jo dropped them?

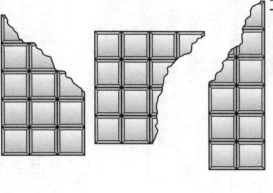

2

Looking for Patterns

Draw the missing shapes in each puzzle.

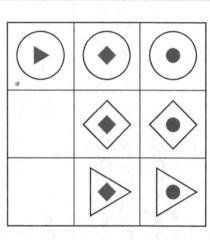

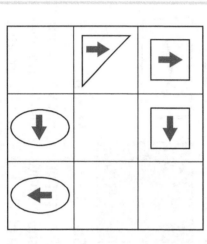

The Puzzler

Look at this square.

BEFORE

Draw 1 line to put 2 ● s in each part.

AFTER

Draw 1 line to put 3 ● s in each part.

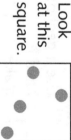

Draw 2 lines to put 2 ◆ s in each part.

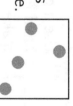

Draw 2 lines to put 3 ▲ s in each part.

Draw 3 lines to put 1 ■ in each part.

Construct

Colouring 4 T shapes fully covers this large 4 × 4 square.

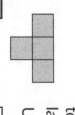

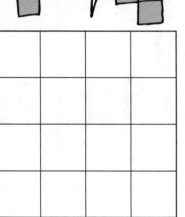

Colour 4 L shapes to fully cover this large 4 × 4 square.
Use 4 different colours.

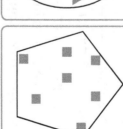

3

The Maths Herald

Name:

Date:

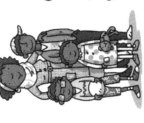

🐝 Let's Investigate

How many people are there in your family?

Count your parents and your brothers and sisters.

Don't forget to count yourself!

Number of people						
2	3	4	5	6	7	8 or more

Put a line (tally mark) in the box in the table that shows the number of people in your family.

Ask other children in your class this question.

Each time, put a line (tally mark) in the table below the number they tell you.

Now count all the tally marks and write each number in this table.

Number of people						
2	3	4	5	6	7	8 or more

In your class, what is the most common size family?

What is the least common size family?

🔬 Focus on Science

☀ sunny ☁ cloudy 🌧 rainy

Keep a record of the weather during the week.

Day of the week	Morning	Afternoon
Monday		
Tuesday		
Wednesday		
Thursday		
Friday		
Saturday		
Sunday		

🐞 The Language of Maths

Look at the table in the 🔬 Focus on Science activity above.

Write some sentences about the weather last week.

tallying

The Language of Maths

How many letters are in your first name?

How many letters are in the first name of some of your classmates?

If you're not sure, ask them.

Write the names in the table.

Number of letters in first name	Names
2	
3	
4	
5	
6	
7	
8	
more than 8	

Focus on Science

Chen has 6 pets.

He has a dog 🐕, a cat 🐈, 2 chickens 🐥🐥, a duck 🦆, and a goldfish 🐠.

He puts his pets into 2 groups.

The ones with wings, 🐥🐥🦆 and the ones with no wings, 🐕🐈🐠.

How else could Chen group his pets?

2

At Home

During the week, keep a record of what you have to eat for your evening meal.

At the end of the week, rewrite your list in order from your favourite meal to your least favourite meal.

Day	Meal
Monday	
Tuesday	
Wednesday	
Thursday	
Friday	
Saturday	
Sunday	

Favourite meal

Least favourite meal

3

S&C Volume 1

The Maths Herald

Name:

Date:

Name	Name
Number	Number

graph

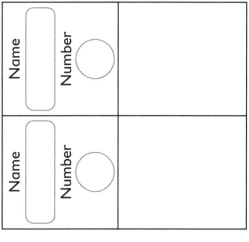

🐞 Let's Investigate

You need:
- 1–6 dice

An activity to do with a friend.

Each of you choose a number on the dice (not the same number).

Write your name and number in the table.

Take turns to roll the dice.

- If the dice number is one of the numbers that either of you chose, make a mark in the correct part of the table.
- If the dice number is not one of your two numbers do nothing.

Keep going until you have rolled the dice about 10 times each.

Whose number was rolled more times?

What would happen if you each chose a different number?

Write about what you have found out.

🐜 The Language of Maths

Write down the first letter of your name.

Make a list of all the things in the classroom, and that you can see outside, that begin with that letter.

Find a friend and look at both lists.

Arrange all the things on both lists into different groups.

Can you organise your lists in different ways?

Hi! I'm Claire.

🏠 At Home

With an adult, take a pencil and paper and find somewhere safe to sit near a road.

Write down the number plates of about 10 cars.

Back home, put the number plates into different groups.

Can you group the number plates in different ways?

Focus on Science

Can you wink?
If you can, which eye can you wink with?
Ask your friends.

Sort them into 4 groups.

- Friends who cannot wink.
- Friends who can wink with only their left eye.
- Friends who can wink with only their right eye.
- Friends who can wink with both eyes.

Discuss with a friend how you are going to show your results.
Which group is biggest? Which group is smallest?

Let's Investigate

What do you think are the 5 most popular meals for the children in your class?
Make a list of the meals.

Now ask all the children in your class which is their favourite meal on your list.
Make a record of how many children like each meal best.

Our favourite meals

Meals	Number of children

Focus on Science

Look around the classroom.
What are different objects made from?
Write the objects in the table.

Wood	Metal	Plastic	Fabric	Other material

Which objects belong in more than one column?

Teacher's notes

Issue 1

Number

Prerequisites for learning

- Read and write numbers to 20 and beyond in numerals and words
- Describe and extend number sequences
- Recognise place value in numbers beyond 20 by reading, writing, counting and comparing numbers up to 100, supported by objects and pictorial representations
- Use knowledge of place value to position numbers on a number track
- Count on or back in ones, twos, fives and tens

Resources

pencil and paper
Resource sheet 2: My notes (optional)
Resource sheet 3: Pupil self assessment booklet (optional)
Tens and Ones abacus and beads (optional)
interlocking cubes

Teaching support

Page 1

Looking for Patterns

- Ensure children realise that each of the circular number sequences goes in a clockwise direction.
- Ask the children for both answers to each pattern (see Answers).
- Ask the children to make their own circular number sequences.

Let's Investigate

- Ensure children understand the term 'digit' and realise that there are 10 digits in our number system: 0, 1, 2, 3, 4, 5, 6, 7, 8 and 9.
- How many ones are there on a 0–20 number track?
- How many digits are there altogether on a 0–50 number track?

Page 2

Let's Investigate

- Ensure the children are familiar with, and are able to accurately read, a Tens and Ones abacus.
- Provide the children with a Tens and Ones abacus to assist them with this activity.
- Tell the children it is possible to make seven different numbers, one of which is given in the Issue, i.e. 24.
- What numbers can you make using six beads on a Hundreds, Tens and Ones abacus?

Looking for Patterns

- Ensure children realise that there are no interlocking cubes in the middle of each shape, just around the four sides.
- The pattern increases by four cubes each time:

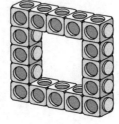

| 8 cubes | 12 cubes | 16 cubes |

- Once the children have identified the pattern, encourage them to work out the number of cubes in shapes with 6, 7, ... sides without using the interlocking cubes.

Page 3

Looking for Patterns

- Some children may have difficulty with the last number sequence that requires them to count backwards to identify the first four numbers in the pattern.
- Ask the children to write down the rule for each number sequence.

The Language of Maths

- If necessary, provide the children with an example:

  My number has 4 tens.

  It is an even number.

  It is greater than 46.

- Tell the children to make up four, rather than three, clues about their number.
- Ask the children to write clues for a number less than 20.
- Ask the children to write clues for a number between 0 and 100.

Page 4

The Puzzler

- Although the answers given on page 96 are the most obvious answers, children may offer other correct answers. The most important aspect of this activity is the justification that children offer as to which hand is different in each row. Therefore, it is important that once the children have completed this activity you discuss with them their reasoning.
- Some children may need help in identifying the answer given for the fourth set of hands (see Answers).

Let's Investigate

- Ensure the children are familiar with, and are able to accurately read, a Tens and Ones abacus.
- Provide the children with a Tens and Ones abacus to assist them with this activity.

AfL

- What is happening to the numbers in this sequence? What patterns do you notice?
- What digits are used to make the number 36? What does the 3 stand for? What about the 6?
- Which digit in the number 84 is in the tens place? What about in the number 215?
- Show me the number 49 on this abacus. What does it mean?
- What patterns did you notice in your shapes? Did you need to make all the shapes to know how many cubes there are in a shape with sides of 6 or 7 cubes long?
- How did you know what numbers belonged in this pattern? What is the rule for the sequence?
- Tell me some of your clues. What were good clues to ask your friend?
- Tell me the odd one out. Why is this hand the odd one out? Can you tell me another hand that belongs in this row? What about a hand that does not belong in this row? Why doesn't it belong?
- What patterns did you notice when you were adding one bead to the abacus?

Answers

Page 1

Looking for Patterns

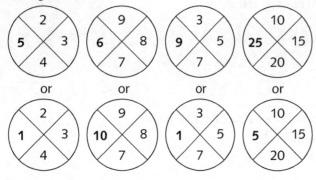

or   or   or   or

Let's Investigate
Altogether there are 32 digits on a 0–20 number track.

Page 2

Let's Investigate
6, 15, 24, 33, 42, 51, 60

Looking for Patterns
In a shape with sides 3 cubes long there are a total of 8 cubes.
In a shape with sides 4 cubes long there are a total of 12 cubes.
In a shape with sides 5 cubes long there are a total of 16 cubes.
In a shape with sides 6 cubes long there are a total of 20 cubes.
In a shape with sides 7 cubes long there are a total of 24 cubes.
The total number of cubes increases by 4 each time an extra cube is added to each side.

Page 3

Looking for Patterns
23, 20, **17**, **14**, **11**, **8**, 5, 2
2, 7, 12, 17, 22, **27**, **32**, **37**, **42**
91, 81, 71, **61**, **51**, **41**, **31**, 21, 11, 1
7, **9**, **11**, **13**, 15, 17, 19, 21, 23

The Language of Maths
Clues will vary.

Page 4

The Puzzler
The following hands are different from the others in the row:

(set of numbers not in the correct counting order)   (set of numbers not all even)

(set of numbers not all multiples of 10)   (set of numbers not all multiples of 5)

Other answers may be possible, however the children must be able to justify their reasoning.

Let's Investigate
13 and 22	28 and 37	34 and 43
22 and 31	19 and 28	47 and 56

Inquisitive ant

place value
The numerical value a digit has due to its position in a number.

Issue 2

Number

Prerequisites for learning

- Read and write numbers to 20 and beyond in numerals and words
- Describe and extend number sequences
- Recognise odd and even numbers
- Compare and order numbers to 20 and beyond
- Say the number that is ten more or less than a given number
- Recognise place value in numbers beyond 20 by reading, writing, counting and comparing numbers up to 100, supported by objects and pictorial representations
- Count on or back in ones, twos, fives and tens

Resources

pencil and paper

Resource sheet 2: My notes (optional)

Resource sheet 3: Pupil self assessment booklet (optional)

set of 1–20 number cards or Resource sheet 4: 1–20 number cards

set of 0–9 digit cards

set of 1–50 number cards (optional)

Tens and Ones abacus and beads (optional)

Teaching support

Page 1

Let's Investigate

- It is possible to make six different two-digit numbers using three different digit cards. For example, using the digits 1, 2 and 3: 12, 13, 21, 23, 31 and 32.
- What if you chose three digit cards? It is possible to make six different three-digit numbers using three different digit cards. For example, 123, 132, 213, 231, 312 and 321.

Looking for Patterns

- Ensure children realise that they are counting the total number of times that the four digit appears. So, for example, in the numbers, **3**4, 35, 36, 37, 38, 39, **4**0, **4**1, **4**2, **4**3 and **44**, the 4 digit appears a total of seven times.
- It is important that children first make an estimate before working out the exact number.
- If necessary, provide the children with a set of 1–50 number cards.
- How many times does the 4 digit appear in the numbers 1 to 100?

Page 2

Looking for Patterns

- Once the children have completed the activity, ask them to do the activity again, but this time starting at 1 rather than 0. What do they notice?
- Ask the children to look at the numbers they have written in each list. Which numbers appear in more than one list? What does this mean?

Let's Investigate

- Ensure the children are familiar with, and are able to accurately read, a Tens and Ones abacus.
- Provide the children with a Tens and Ones abacus to assist them with this activity.

Page 3

Looking for Patterns

- Ask the children to write down the rule for each number sequence.
- Ask the children to write similar number sequences of their own for a friend to complete.

Let's Investigate

- Children need to confidently and quickly identify odd and even numbers to 100 for this activity.
- Prior to setting the children off to work independently on this activity, discuss it with them, ensuring that they understand what is required.
- There are two aspects to this activity. Firstly, the children carrying out the investigation – making two-digit numbers, reversing the digits to make another two-digit number, and identifying whether the two numbers made are odd or even numbers. The second part of this activity requires the children to answer the four questions and draw conclusions as to which odd / even numbers stay odd / even when the digits are reversed, and which do not. Therefore, in order to complete the second part of this activity, it is recommended that you remind the children of the need to keep a record of their results in the first part of the activity.

Page 4

The Language of Maths

- If there are insufficient packs of 1–20 number cards, provide the children with the two sheets from Resource sheet 4: 1–20 number cards.

- Introduce the children to an alternative version of the game:

  Before they start:

  – children begin by laying out the 1–20 number cards in order face up on the table.

  They take turns to:

  – secretly choose one of the rules on the flags

  – take all the cards that match the rule and place them in a different line.

  Can the other player guess the rule?

  Play six rounds: three rounds where each child is choosing the rule.

AfL

- How many different two-digit numbers were you able to make? How many different three-digit numbers? How do you know that you have made all the different numbers possible?
- How did you work out how many times you write the digit 4 in all the numbers from 1 to 50? Can you work out how many times you would write the digit 4 in all the numbers from 50 to 100? What patterns did you notice?
- What patterns did you notice when you counted on in steps of 2 / 3 / 4 / 5 from 0? How would the patterns be different if you started at 1 rather than 0?
- What patterns did you notice when you were subtracting one bead from the abacus?
- What is happening to the numbers in this sequence? What patterns do you notice? What is the rule? What are the next two numbers?
- What did you find out that happens to odd and even two-digit numbers when you changed their digits around?
- What were good questions to ask your partner? Why was this a good question?

Answers

Page 1

Let's Investigate
Numbers will vary. However, there should be six different two-digit numbers.

Looking for Patterns
The 4 digit appears 15 times in the numbers 1 to 50: 4, 14, 24, 34, 40, 41, 42, 43, 44 (twice), 45, 46, 47, 48 and 49.

Page 2

Looking for Patterns
Jumping on in steps of 2: 2, 4, 6, 8, 10, 12, 14, 16, 18, 20, 22, 24, 26, 28, 30.
Jumping on in steps of 3: 3, 6, 9, 12, 15, 18, 21, 24, 27, 30.
Jumping on in steps of 4: 4, 8, 12, 16, 20, 24, 28.
Jumping on in steps of 5: 5, 10, 15, 20, 25, 30.

Let's Investigate

19 and 28	22 and 31	34 and 43
7 and 16	16 and 25	43 and 52

Page 3

Looking for Patterns
2, 4, 6, 8, **10**, **12**, **14**
5, 10, 15, 20, **25**, **30**, **35**
1, 4, 7, 10, **13**, **16**, **19**
2, 9, 16, 23, **30**, **37**, **44**

Let's Investigate
An even number stays even when both its digits are even numbers, e.g. 42 and 24.
An even number becomes an odd number when its tens digit is an odd number, e.g. 36 and 63.
An odd number stays odd when both its digits are odd numbers, e.g. 57 and 75.
An odd number becomes an even number when its tens digit is an even number, e.g. 81 and 18.

Page 4

The Language of Maths
No answer required.

Inquisitive ant

digit
The numerals 0 to 9.

Number

Prerequisites for learning

- Read and write numbers to 20 and beyond in numerals and words
- Describe and extend number sequences
- Recognise odd and even numbers
- Use ordinal numbers in different contexts
- Compare and order numbers to 20 and beyond
- Count on or back in ones, twos, fives and tens
- Solve logic puzzles

Resources

pencil and paper
Resource sheet 2: My notes (optional)
Resource sheet 3: Pupil self assessment booklet (optional)
Resource sheet 5: 1–9 grid puzzle

Teaching support

Page 1

Looking for Patterns

- There are two aspects to this activity. Firstly, completing each of the number sequences. Secondly, commenting on the fact that the number in each of the large shapes is the same whether counting on or back.
- Ask the children to make a similar number sequence of their own, e.g.

  0, 3, 6, 9, 12, 15 , 18, 21, 24, 27, 30.

Let's Investigate

- Tell the children that there are four different combinations of cars and motorbikes that Mike could have seen. Can they find them all?

Page 2

Looking for Patterns

- Ask the children to write the rule for each number sequence.
- Ask the children to write the next three numbers in each sequence.

Sports Update

- Ensure the children have had some experience of logic puzzles before attempting this activity.
- Also ensure that the children are familiar with the terms: 'between', 'even' and 'largest'.

Page 3

Looking for Patterns

- This activity introduces children to the idea that sequences are not just about numbers, but can be about almost anything, including shapes and letters.
- Ask the children to substitute the initial letter of each item in the sequence with digits or shapes, e.g. o, b, b, o, b, b, o, … could become 1, 2, 2, 1, 2, 2, 1… or ☆, ◇, ◇, ☆, ◇, ◇, ☆, … Encourage the children to be as imaginative as possible.

The Puzzler

- Ensure children are familiar with ordinal numbers and their abbreviations.

Page 4

The Puzzler

- Ensure that the children are familiar with the terms: 'digit', 'odd', 'even', 'less than', 'more than', 'between', 'half' and 'largest'.

- If necessary, work with the children to complete clues B and C.

- Tell the children to look carefully at all the clues before filling in the grid. Discuss with them how there are two different types of clues. Some of the clues clearly say which digit to write in which box, e.g. Clue C: 'This digit is half of 12'; while other clues lead to several possible digits, e.g. Clue A: 'This digit is odd'. Encourage the children to begin by looking for all the first type of clues, before then using the second type of clues to work out what digits belong in the remaining boxes on the grid.

- Direct children to clues B, C, E, G and I. This will lead them to five of the numbers. Clues D and F, and then A and H will then give them the remaining four numbers.

- Children need to have completed this activity before starting on the following activity (🐜 The Language of Maths).

The Language of Maths

- Children need to have completed the previous activity (🐜 The Puzzler) before starting on this activity.

- Ensure children realise that they write the digits 1 to 9, in any order, on the grid in the Issue (and keep it secret from their partner). They use Resource sheet 5: 1–9 grid puzzle, to write the clues for their friend.

- Children use an additional copy of Resource sheet 5: 1–9 grid puzzle, and turn the digits 1–9 into nine two-digit numbers. They then write clues for these numbers, e.g.

16
24 31
44 52 60
78 88 96

AfL

- What do you notice about the numbers you wrote in the three large shapes?

- What did Mike see? Could he have seen anything different?

- How did you know that that number belonged in this number pattern?

- How did you work out the answer to this problem / puzzle?

- What is the rule for this pattern? How do you know?

- Which clues were easy? Which clues were a little tricky?

- Tell me one of the clues that you used for your puzzle. Was it a good clue? Why / Why not?

Answers

Page 1

Looking for Patterns

Let's Investigate

Accept any of the following:

- 3 cars
- 2 cars and 2 motorbikes
- 1 car and 4 motorbikes
- 6 motorbikes

Page 2

Looking for Patterns

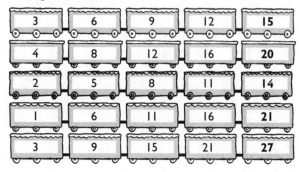

Sports Update

Lee wears number 3.
Mark wears number 2.
Amy wears number 1.
Josh wears number 4.

Page 3

Looking for Patterns

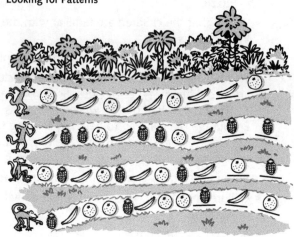

The Puzzler

Page 4

The Puzzler

A 5	B 1	C 6
D 8	E 7	F 3
G 2	H 4	I 9

The Language of Maths

Grids and clues will vary.

Inquisitive ant

even number

A whole number that can be divided exactly by 2.

Issue 4

Number

Prerequisites for learning

- Read and write numbers to 20 and beyond in numerals and words
- Describe and extend number sequences
- Recognise odd and even numbers
- Use knowledge of place value to position numbers on a number track
- Use ordinal numbers in different contexts
- Compare and order numbers to 20 and beyond
- Count on or back in ones, twos, fives and tens
- Understand and use the basic functions of a calculator
- Solve logic puzzles

Resources

pencil and paper
Resource sheet 2: My notes (optional)
Resource sheet 3: Pupil self assessment booklet (optional)
Resource sheet 6: Dogs, cats and chickens
scissors
glue
large sheet of paper
counters, cubes or similar (optional)
calculator
1–100 number square

Teaching support

Page 1

Looking for Patterns

- This activity introduces children to the idea that sequences are not just about numbers, but can be about almost anything, including animals.

- If necessary, work with the children to create another pattern using two dogs, two cats and two chickens, e.g.

- Encourage children to record their patterns in written form using appropriate mathematical symbols.

Technology Today

- Discuss with the children each of the calculator patterns in the Issue. Ensure they realise that the first pattern shows a series of digits that have been repeated to form a pattern. Whereas the second pattern shows a sequence of numbers counting on in steps of two.
- Ensure the children record their number patterns / sequences.

Page 2

Looking for Patterns

- Suggest the children number the unnumbered divisions in each of the number lines.
- Ask the children to write down the steps that each of the number lines go up in, e.g.

Steps of 1   Steps of 2

The Puzzler

- Tell the children to look carefully at all the clues before writing the numbers on the shirts. Discuss with them how there are two different types of clues. Some of the clues clearly say which digit to write on which shirt, e.g. clues 1 and 2; while other clues lead to several possible digits, e.g. clues 3, 4 and 5. Encourage the children to begin by looking for all the first type of clues, before then using the second type of clues to work out what digits belong on the remaining shirts.
- Direct children to clues 1 and 2. This will lead them to two of the numbers. Clues 3, 4 and 5 will then give them the remaining three numbers.

Page 3

Looking for Patterns

- If necessary, provide the children with counters, cubes or some other appropriate resource to assist them in working out the answer.
- When the children have completed the activity, discuss with them the strategies they used for working out the answer to the problem.

- What if there were 10 cans in the bottom row of the stack?

Let's Investigate

- Ensure children realise that they need to describe the combination of people and dogs that Toby sees, as well as the total number of legs.

- Suggest the children draw a diagram to help them work out the answer to the problem.
- Tell the children that there are five different combinations of people and dogs that Toby could have seen. Can they find them all?

Page 4

Looking for Patterns

- Ensure children realise that there are many different combinations of numbers possible. The children are not expected to identify all of these possible combinations.

- What if there were seven cards rather than five?
  Do the children realise that the order of the last three cards is always 7, 8 and 9?

Looking for Patterns

- If necessary, provide the children with a 1–100 number square to help them count on and back from the start number.
- Ask the children to suggest other numbers that Sunita would say, if appropriate, including numbers greater than 100.
- Ask the children to suggest numbers that Connor would say.
- The most important part of this activity is the children's ability to explain why, or why not, the number is included in the count. Encourage the children to give as thorough an explanation as possible.

AfL

- Describe one of your patterns to me.
- Tell me one of your repeating calculator patterns. Why do these numbers make a pattern?
- How do you know that this is the missing number? What is happening to these numbers? What is the rule?
- How did you work out the answer to this problem / puzzle?
- Which clues were really helpful?
- What did Toby see? Could he have seen anything different?
- Tell me what the other four cards might be. Is this the right order? Show me what the cards might be, but not in the right order smallest to largest, and see if I can put them in the right order. Am I right?
- Explain to me why Sunita is correct. Tell me another number Sunita would say.
- Explain to me why Connor is not correct. Tell me a number that he would say.

Answers

Page 1

Looking for Patterns
Patterns will vary.

Technology Today
Patterns will vary.

Page 2

Looking for Patterns

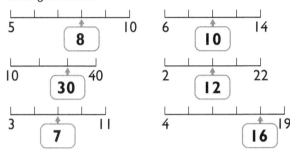

The Puzzler

Page 3

Looking for Patterns
Gavin needs to add another 15 cans.
There will be 36 cans in the stack altogether.

Let's Investigate
Accept any of the following:
- 4 people and 8 legs.
- 3 people, 1 dog and 10 legs.
- 2 people, 2 dogs and 12 legs.
- 1 person, 3 dogs and 14 legs.
- 4 dogs and 16 legs.

Page 4

Looking for Patterns
Answers will vary.

Looking for Patterns
When counting on in fives from 5 Sunita would say the number 100 because 100 is a multiple of 5.
When counting back in twos from 32 Connor would not say the number 13 because unlike 32, 13 is not an even number / multiple of 2.

Inquisitive ant   divide
Separate into equal pieces or groups.

Addition

Prerequisites for learning

- Describe simple patterns and relationships involving numbers
- Derive and recall all addition number bonds to 20
- Use knowledge of number bonds and operations to estimate and check answers to calculations
- Use concrete objects and pictorial representations to support the addition of a one-digit number or a multiple of 10 to a one-digit number
- Add more than two numbers
- Read, write and interpret mathematical statements involving addition (+) and equals (=) signs

Resources

pencil and paper
Resource sheet 2: My notes (optional)
Resource sheet 3: Pupil self assessment booklet (optional)
set of 0–9 digit cards (optional)
counters
0–9 dice

Teaching support

Page 1

The Puzzler

- Tell the children that there is more than one possible solution for each of the puzzles. Can they find them?

Money Matters

- Before setting the children off to work independently on this activity, discuss with them the parts of teddy's body that you might put a price on, e.g. ears, eyes, nose, mouth, head, body, arms and legs.
- If teddy cost exactly £1, what would be the price for each of the different parts of teddy?

Page 2

Let's Investigate

- Provide the children with a set of 1–9 digit cards.
- Tell the children that next-door numbers are *called consecutive numbers*.
- Ask the children to investigate what happens if you add three consecutive (next-door) numbers.
- Once the children have completed the activity, arrange them into pairs or groups to discuss what they noticed.

The Puzzler

- Ensure the children understand how the grids work.
- Also ensure the children have completed this activity before starting on the first 🐝 The Puzzler activity on page 3.
- Ask the children to find the total of the two numbers in the circles in the third column, and the sum of the two numbers in the circles in the bottom row. What do they notice?

1	3	(4)
1	4	(5)
(2)	(7)	**9**

Page 3

The Puzzler

- Children need to have completed 🐝 The Puzzler activity on page 2 before starting on this activity.
- Different solutions are possible. Once children have found one solution to each of the problems ask them to find another solution.
- Ask the children to write similar problems for a friend to solve.

The Puzzler

- Ask the children to write some 4-pointed star problems of their own, either using a centre number chosen by the teacher, or choosing the centre number for themselves.
- Ask the children to write some 3-pointed star or 5-pointed star problems, e.g.

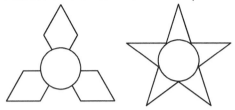

Page 4

Let's Investigate

- Discuss with the children how the following calculations are considered the same:

  5 + 4 + 1

  5 + 1 + 4

  4 + 5 + 1

  4 + 1 + 5

  1 + 5 + 4

  1 + 4 + 5

- Allow the children to use counters.
- Encourage the children to complete the activity without the use of counters.

Let's Investigate

- You may wish to tell the children that if they roll the same number more than once to roll the dice again.

- Encourage the children to write the numbers they have written in the large shapes at the top of the activity, in the smaller shapes in each of the calculations.
- When writing their own subtraction number sentences ensure the children realise that the first shape must have a larger number than the second shape, i.e.

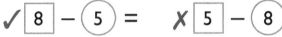

- Suggest the children make multiplication calculations.

AfL

- How did you work out the answer to this problem / puzzle?
- How did you know that the numbers have to go here? Could they go anywhere else?
- How much does your teddy cost? How much are his arms worth? Is this more or less than the price of his legs? How did you work out how much your teddy costs altogether?
- What can you tell me about the sum / total of pairs of next-door numbers? Is there some rule to always help you work out these answers quickly and easily?
- Look at the two numbers in the circles in this column of the puzzle. What is the sum / total of these two numbers? Now look at the two numbers in the circles in the bottom row of this puzzle. What is the sum / total of these two numbers? What do you notice?
- How did you work out which numbers belonged in the grid?
- Is there more than one answer to this problem / puzzle? What might it be? Are there any more answers / solutions?
- What number did you roll to write in the square? What about the circle? What is the sum / total of these two numbers? What is the difference between these two numbers? What is the answer if you times / multiply these two numbers together?

Answers

Page 1

The Puzzler

 Other solutions are possible.

 Other solutions are possible.

Money Matters
Prices and totals will vary.

Page 2

Let's Investigate
Observations will vary but may include:
- The sum of pairs of consecutive (next-door) numbers is always an odd number.
- The sum is double the smaller number plus one.
- The sum is double the larger number minus one.

The Puzzler

Page 3

The Puzzler

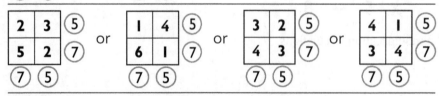

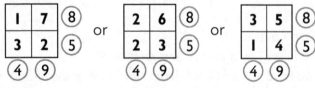

The Puzzler
Numbers around the stars will vary.

Page 4

Let's Investigate

10 + 0 + 0	9 + 1 + 0	8 + 2 + 0	7 + 3 + 0
	8 + 1 + 1	6 + 2 + 2	4 + 3 + 3
	7 + 1 + 2	5 + 2 + 3	
	6 + 1 + 3	4 + 2 + 4	
	5 + 1 + 4		

6 + 4 + 0   5 + 5 + 0   Calculations may vary, e.g.
0 + 0 + 10 or 0 + 10 + 0

Let's Investigate
Numbers, calculations and answers will vary.

Inquisitive ant

total
The whole of something. A word used to describe addition.

Issue 6

Addition

Prerequisites for learning

- Describe simple patterns and relationships involving numbers
- Solve a puzzle or problem in the context of money
- Derive and recall all addition number bonds to 20
- Use knowledge of number facts and operations to estimate and check answers to calculations
- Add more than two numbers
- Read, write and interpret mathematical statements involving addition (+) and equals (=) signs

Resources

pencil and paper
Resource sheet 2: My notes (optional)
Resource sheet 3: Pupil self assessment booklet (optional)
interlocking cubes
calculator (optional)
1p, 2p, 5p and 10p coins (optional)
coloured pencils

Teaching support

Page 1

Sports Update

- Ensure children realise that the number of skittles Tammy knocked down matches the number of blank skittles.
- For the scores of 15 and 14, tell the children that there are three different possible answers for each score. Can they find them all? For the score of 17, there are two different possible answers. Can the children find both of these?

Page 2

Let's Investigate

- This practical activity reinforces children's recall of pairs of numbers that total 10. Once the children have written several number sentences, ask them to look carefully at what they have done. Can they use these facts to help them identify other pairs of numbers that total 10?
- Ensure the children realise that, for example, 4 + 6 and 6 + 4 are the same complement of 10.

Sports Update

- Ensure children realise that no team can have two players with the same number, e.g.

Although the five numbers total 25, the team has two number 6 players.

- If necessary, work through the first problem with the children, i.e.

2 + 4 + 6 = 12

25 − ☐ = 12

☐ = 13

Therefore we need to look for two numbers that total 13, i.e. 5 + 8 (although 6 + 7 = 13, this is not correct as the team already has a number 6 player).

- Allow the children to use a calculator.

Page 3

Money Matters

- Provide the children with 1p, 2p, 5p and 10p coins.
- Tell the children that each row, column and diagonal must have a 1p, a 2p, a 5p and a 10p coin.

Sports Update

- Allow the children to use a calculator.
- What if you were allowed to travel sideways as well as up and down and diagonally, landing on no more than eight numbers? Which route scores the most points?

Page 4

Let's Investigate

- This highly practical activity reinforces children's understanding that more than two numbers can be added together and also the complements of 12.
- Ensure children realise that each of the numbers in the number sentence in the Issue refers to one of the rows in the shape.
- The most important aspect of this activity is writing the number sentences.

The Puzzler

- Tell the children that there is more than one possible solution for each of the puzzles. Can they find them?

AfL

- How did Tammy score 15 points? Is there another way that Tammy could have scored 15 points?
- Tell me one of your number sentences.
- Which number is missing from this sports kit? How did you work out that it was that number that was missing?
- How did you solve this puzzle?
- Which route scored the most / least points? Are you sure that this is the route with the smallest / largest total?
- Look at this shape made from interlocking cubes. What is the number sentence that tells me how many cubes I have used in each row and how many cubes there are altogether?
- How do you know that the numbers belong here? Is there another solution to this puzzle?

Answers

Page 1

Sports Update

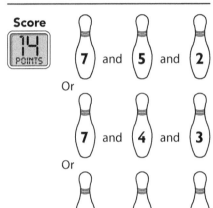

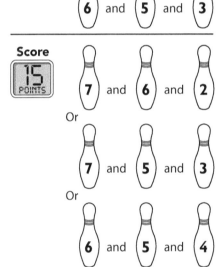

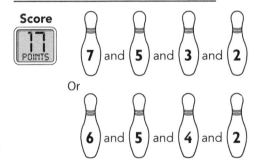

Page 2

Let's Investigate

1 + 9

2 + 8

3 + 7

4 + 6

5 + 5

Sports Update

The missing numbers from the teams are:

5 and 8

6 and 7

4 and 9

Page 3

Money Matters

Other solutions are possible.

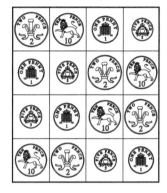

Sports Update

Most points – 37 points   Least points – 14 points

4	2	1	6	3
5	3	7	8	4
7	9	5	6	8
2	8	7	4	1
7	1	3	5	2

4	2	1	6	3
5	3	7	8	4
7	9	5	6	8
2	8	7	4	1
7	1	3	5	2

Page 4

Let's Investigate

Number sentences will vary.

The Puzzler

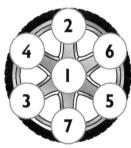   

Other solutions   Other solutions
are possible.   are possible.

Inquisitive ant

number sentence

A mathematical expression about the number or size of something, that uses numbers and symbols.

Issue 7

Subtraction

Prerequisites for learning

- Describe simple patterns and relationships involving numbers
- Derive and recall all addition number bonds and related subtraction facts within 20
- Understand subtraction as 'take away' and find a 'difference' by counting up
- Use knowledge of number facts and operations to estimate and check answers to calculations
- Use concrete objects and pictorial representations to support the subtraction of a one-digit number from a one-digit or two-digit number
- Read, write and interpret mathematical statements involving addition (+), subtraction (−) and equals (=) signs

Resources

pencil and paper

Resource sheet 2: My notes (optional)

Resource sheet 3: Pupil self assessment booklet (optional)

set of double-5 dominoes

20 counters

container

Teaching support

Page 1

The Arts Roundup

- This activity reinforces children's understanding that more than one smaller number can be subtracted from a larger number.
- Encourage the children to write a number sentence showing how many paintings Louis did not sell, i.e. $16 - 7 - 5 = 4$.

Looking for Patterns

- There are 21 dominoes in a set of double-5 dominoes.
- Make sure the children understand that the difference is between the two touching halves of each domino.
- Tell the children that there is more than one possible solution. Can they find them?
- What if the difference between touching dominoes was 2?

Page 2

The Puzzler

- Ensure the children understand how these puzzles work.
- Children need to have completed this activity before starting on the first 🐜 The Puzzler activity on page 3.

Looking for Patterns

- Ask the children to write all the subtraction number facts for another number, e.g. 6. Are the patterns for this number similar to those for the subtraction number facts for 10?

  $6 - 0 = 6$ $6 - 1 = 5$ $6 - 2 = 4$ $6 - 3 = 3$ $6 - 4 = 2$ $6 - 5 = 1$ $6 - 6 = 0$

- Ask the children to write all the addition number facts for 10 (or another number). How are the patterns for the addition number facts the same as for the subtraction number facts? How are they different?

  $0 + 10 = 10$ $1 + 9 = 10$ $2 + 8 = 10$ $3 + 7 = 10$ $4 + 6 = 10$ $5 + 5 = 10$

  $6 + 4 = 10$ $7 + 3 = 10$ $8 + 2 = 10$ $9 + 1 = 10$ $10 + 0 = 10$

Page 3

The Puzzler

- Children need to have completed 🐜 The Puzzler activity on page 2 before starting on this activity.
- If necessary, work through the first question with the children, i.e. 7 – 2 = 5.

The Puzzler

- This activity reinforces children's understanding that more than one smaller number can be subtracted from a larger number.
- Ensure children understand that they must subtract the two numbers on the balls on the back of each lorry from the number on the lorry's cab.
- When discussing this activity with the children, use a variety of mathematical terms for subtraction, such as 'take away', 'minus' and 'less'.

Page 4

The Puzzler

- As the children play the game, after each turn, encourage them to say the related subtraction calculation, e.g.
  - *There are 12 counters in the pile and I'm going to take away 2. 12 subtract 2 is 10.*
  - *There are 10 counters. One less than 10 is 9.*
- As they reach the end of the pile, do the children realise that if they are the player that takes away one (or two) counter(s) so that there are three counters remaining, then they will win?

What's the Problem?

- The most important aspect of this activity is the reasoning that children offer as to why Karen wrote 7 – 2 = 9.

AfL

- How did you work out the answer to this problem? What is the number sentence you need to do to work out this answer?
- There is more than one solution to this puzzle. Can you work out another solution?
- Tell me the number sentence for this hourglass.
- What patterns do you notice in this list of subtraction number facts for 10? Do you think it is similar for the subtraction number facts for 9 or 8? What patterns do you think there are in the addition number facts for 10?
- What was a good strategy / way to help you win the game?

Answers

Page 1

The Arts Roundup

16 – 7 – 5 = 4
Louis did not sell four paintings.

Looking for Patterns

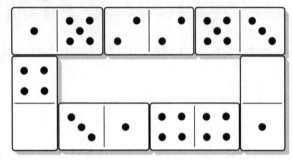

Other solutions are possible.

Page 2

The Puzzler

6 – 3 = 3	5 – 1 = 4
8 – 3 = 5	7 – 4 = 3
10 – 2 = 8	9 – 6 = 3

Looking for Patterns

Explanations of patterns will vary.

Page 3

The Puzzler

7 – 2 = 5	5 – 3 = 2
5 – 4 = 1	6 – 2 = 4
7 – 0 = 7	10 – 5 = 5

The Puzzler

11 – 2 – 5 = 4
15 – 6 – 3 = 6
17 – 5 – 8 = 4
13 – 7 – 2 = 4
16 – 9 – 6 = 1
20 – 7 – 8 = 5

Page 4

The Puzzler

Strategies for winning the game will vary.

What's the Problem?

7 – 2 = 9
Karen calculated 7 + 2 rather than 7 – 2.
The correct answer is 7 – 2 = 5.

Inquisitive ant

subtract
Take away a number or amount from another number or amount.

Issue 8

Subtraction

Prerequisites for learning

- Describe simple patterns and relationships involving numbers
- Derive and recall all addition number bonds and related subtraction facts within 20
- Understand subtraction as 'take away' and find a 'difference' by counting up
- Use knowledge of number facts and operations to estimate and check answers to calculations
- Use concrete objects and pictorial representations to support the subtraction of a one-digit number from a one-digit or two-digit number
- Read, write and interpret mathematical statements involving subtraction (−) and equals (=) signs

Resources

pencil and paper
Resource sheet 2: My notes (optional)
Resource sheet 3: Pupil self assessment booklet (optional)
1–6 dice
double-6 dominoes
counters

Teaching support

Page 1

The Puzzler

- Ensure that children understand subtraction as both 'take away' and find a 'difference' by counting up.
- When discussing this activity with the children, use a variety of mathematical terms for subtraction, such as 'difference', 'subtract', 'take away', 'minus' and 'less'.

The Puzzler

- As with the previous activity, ensure that children understand subtraction as both 'take away' and find a 'difference' by counting up.

Page 2

Let's Investigate

- Ensure children understand that:
  - for questions written like this, the two numbers are side-by-side on the grid;

9	

  - for questions written like this, the two numbers are one above the other.

10

- Children need to have completed this activity before starting on the following 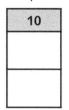 Let's Investigate activity.

Let's Investigate

- Children need to have completed the previous Let's Investigate activity before starting on this activity.
- Ask children to look for all the pairs of numbers that have a difference of 2, 4, 6, 7 and 11, as there are at least two pairs of numbers on the grid that have a difference of each of these numbers.

Page 3

Let's Investigate

- It is recommended that children have completed this activity before starting on the following Let's Investigate activity and The Puzzler game on page 4.
- This activity involves the children finding all the possible differences between two 1–6 dice. This then leads into the next activity, where children find all the possible differences between the numbers of dots on a set of dominoes. Children need to know this information before playing The Puzzler game on page 4.
- Tell the children that there are six possible differences between two 1–6 dice.

Let's Investigate

- It is recommended that children have completed the previous Let's Investigate activity before starting on this activity and The Puzzler game on page 4.
- This activity involves the children finding all the possible differences between the numbers of dots on a set of dominoes. Children need to know this information before playing The Puzzler game on page 4. Therefore, ensure the children have successfully answered this question before they start on The Puzzler game on page 4.
- Tell the children that there are seven possible differences between the numbers of dots on a set of dominoes.

Page 4

The Puzzler

- Children need to have successfully completed the second Let's Investigate activity on page 3 before playing this game. Therefore, ensure the children realise that it is the numbers 0, 1, 2, 3, 4, 5 and 6 that need to go in the boxes at the top of the page.
- Ensure children are familiar with the rules of the game before setting them off to play it independently. You may wish to spend a few minutes playing the game with the children to get them started.

AfL

- What is the difference between these two numbers?
- How did you work out the difference?
- Can you tell me another pair of numbers that have a difference of 3 / 6?
- What about using some larger numbers not on the grid?
- What are all the possible differences between two 1–6 dice? What about between the dots on a set of dominoes?

Answers

Page 1

The Puzzler
26 – 4 = 22
57 – 6 = 51
29 – 7 = 22
73 – 9 = 64
87 – 10 = 77
45 – 8 = 37

The Puzzler

10	4	2	15	21
8	9	5	7	13
2	12	3	9	17
6	5	10	7	14
9	11	1	13	16

1 is the number that does not have a ring around it and is not coloured in.

Page 2

Let's Investigate

2	
1	3

7	
4	11

6	
9	15

10
5
15

4
3
7

11
13
2

6
7
13

Other answers are possible.

Let's Investigate
Numbers with a difference of 9:

10	1

14	5

15	6

Page 3

Let's Investigate
There are six possible differences between two 1–6 dice:
0, 1, 2, 3, 4 and 5.

Let's Investigate
There are seven possible differences between the numbers of dots on a set of dominoes: 0, 1, 2, 3, 4, 5 and 6.

Page 4

The Puzzler
The numbers in the seven boxes at the top of the game should be: 0, 1, 2, 3, 4, 5 and 6.

Inquisitive ant

difference
The amount by which numbers or amounts differ. The remainder left after the subtraction of one number or quantity from another.

Multiplication

Prerequisites for learning

- Describe simple patterns and relationships involving numbers
- Solve a puzzle or problem in the context of money
- Count on or back in ones, twos, fives and tens
- Solve practical problems that involve combining groups of 2, 5 or 10
- Use knowledge of number facts and operations to estimate and check answers to calculations
- Use concrete objects, pictorial representations, arrays and related vocabulary to support multiplication

Resources

pencil and paper

Resource sheet 2: My notes (optional)

Resource sheet 3: Pupil self assessment booklet (optional)

Resource sheet 7: Bookshelf

Resource sheet 19: 2 cm squared paper

scissors

counters

ruler

Teaching support

Page 1

Looking for Patterns

- This activity reinforces children's ability to count on in steps of ten, and recognise the multiples of ten.
- It is recommended that children complete this activity before starting on the following 🐜 Looking for Patterns activity and the 🐜 Looking for Patterns activity on page 3.

Looking for Patterns

- This activity introduces children to counting on in steps of four, and recognising the multiples of four.
- It is recommended that children have completed the previous 🐜 Looking for Patterns activity before starting on this activity. It is also recommended that children complete this activity before starting on the 🐜 Looking for Patterns activity on page 3.

Page 2

Let's Investigate

- This highly practical activity reinforces children's understanding of multiplication as arrays and the commutative law as it applies to multiplication, i.e. $2 \times 5 = 5 \times 2$.
- If appropriate, encourage the children to write a related multiplication number sentence on the rectangular array that they cut out. Can they write two multiplication number sentences for each array, e.g. $5 \times 2 = 10$ and $2 \times 5 = 10$?
- Ask the children to cut out square arrays and write the related multiplication number sentence. What do they notice? If appropriate, you may wish to introduce to the children the term 'square number'.
- Once the children have completed this activity, if they have also completed the 🐝 Let's Investigate activity on page 1 of Issue 10 – Multiplication, discuss with them the similarities between these two activities.

What's the Problem?

- This activity reinforces children's ability to count on in steps of five and ten.
- Suggest that children draw a simple picture of all seven birds with their wings outspread and then count up in tens.
- What if there were 9 / 10 / 12 … birds? How many spots would the birds have altogether?
- What if each bird had 3 / 4 spots on each wing? How many spots would the seven birds have altogether?

Page 3

Looking for Patterns

- This activity reinforces children's ability to count on in steps of 20, and recognise the multiples of 20.
- Discuss with the children the patterns they notice between the multiples of 2 and the multiples of 20.
- It is recommended that children have completed the two Looking for Patterns activities on page 1 before starting on this activity.

At Home

- Once the children have completed the investigation, ensure that there is an opportunity in class for pairs or groups of children to discuss their results.
- Do the children realise that there are two ways of calculating the number of toes, i.e. 10 times the number of people or five times the number of feet?

Page 4

Let's Investigate

- This activity reinforces children's understanding of multiplication as repeated addition.
- For this activity, children do not need the 12 toys at the bottom of Resource sheet 7: Bookshelf. It is recommended that before you give each child their copy of the sheet, you cut off this part of the Resource sheet.

Money Matters

- Provide each child with a sheet of 2 cm squared paper (Resource sheet 19). Ask them to draw their own shapes, carefully divide each shape into sections of equal size and assign a value to one of the sections in each shape. They then give their shapes to a friend to work out the total value of each shape.

AfL

- Describe one of your rectangles to me. What is the number sentence for this rectangle? Can you tell me another number sentence to describe this rectangle?
- How did you work out the answer to this problem?
- What patterns did you notice? How did this help you work out the answer to the problem?
- What steps were you counting in when you worked out the answer to this problem?
- What are four lots of ten? How would you write this as a number sentence?
- What is the total value of this shape? How did you work it out?

Answers

Page 1

Looking for Patterns
10, 20, 30, 40, 50, 60, …
Explanation of patterns will vary. However, all the numbers are multiples of 10.

Looking for Patterns
4, 8, 12, 16, 20, 24, …
Explanation of patterns will vary. However, all the numbers are multiples of 4.

Page 2

Let's Investigate
Results of the investigation will vary.

What's the Problem?
One bird has 10 spots.
Seven birds have a total of 70 spots.

Page 3

Looking for Patterns
20, 40, 60, 80, 100, 120, …
Explanation of patterns will vary. However, all the numbers are multiples of 20.

At Home
Answers will vary.

Page 4

Let's Investigate
4, 8, 12, 16, …

Money Matters

| 6p | 20p | 4p | 25p | 60p |

Inquisitive ant

× The symbol for multiplication.

Issue 10

Multiplication

Prerequisites for learning

- Describe simple patterns and relationships involving numbers
- Count on or back in ones, twos, fives and tens and use this knowledge to derive the multiples of 2, 5 and 10
- Solve practical problems that involve combining groups of 2, 5 or 10
- Use knowledge of number facts and operations to estimate and check answers to calculations
- Use concrete objects, pictorial representations, arrays and related vocabulary to support multiplication

Resources

pencil and paper

Resource sheet 2: My notes (optional)

Resource sheet 3: Pupil self assessment booklet (optional)

Resource sheet 19: 2 cm squared paper

counters

coloured pencil

1–6 dice

buttons

Teaching support

Page 1

Let's Investigate

- This highly practical activity reinforces children's understanding of multiplication as arrays and the commutative law as it applies to multiplication, i.e. $4 \times 3 = 3 \times 4$.
- As the children complete an array, suggest they draw circles on the grid paper to represent their counters and record the array that they make.

- If appropriate, encourage the children to write a related multiplication number sentence on the rectangular array that they make. Can they write two multiplication number sentences for each array, e.g. $4 \times 3 = 12$ and $3 \times 4 = 12$.

- Ask the children to make square arrays and write the related multiplication number sentence. What do they notice? If appropriate, you may wish to introduce to the children the term 'square number'.
- Once the children have completed this activity, if they have also completed the 🐜 Let's Investigate activity on page 2 of Issue 9 – Multiplication, discuss with them the similarities between these two activities.

What's the Problem?

- If children are having difficulty working out the answer to the last part of the question, point out that they can work out how many eggs the extra four hens lay, and then add this number to the total they worked out in the first part of the question.

Page 2

The Language of Maths

- This activity introduces children to the concept of multiples, and in particular the multiples of 2, 5 and 10. It also provides an opportunity for children to use their knowledge of these multiples to apply it to working out the multiples of 3 and 4.
- Children need to have completed, and understood, this activity before starting on the second 🐜 Looking for Patterns activity on page 3 and the 🐜 Looking for Patterns game on page 4.

What's the Problem?

- Ensure children understand that although sheep and chickens have different types of legs, they can add them together.
- If children are experiencing difficulty, suggest they draw a simple picture of the animals showing their legs.

Page 3

Looking for Patterns

- If children have difficulty counting back, suggest that they work out the pattern and then start from the end and count on by that amount until they reach the next given number in the sequence.

- Ask the children to write down the rule for each number sequence.
- Ask the children to write down what number belongs before each of the first numbers given in each sequence, i.e. zero in the case of the first sequence: 0, 2, 4, 6, 8, 10, 12, 14.

Looking for Patterns

- Children need to have completed, and understood The Language of Maths activity on page 2 before starting on this activity. They also need to have completed this activity before starting on the Looking for Patterns game on page 4.

- Once the children have completed this activity, arrange them into pairs or groups to compare and discuss their completed 1–100 number squares. What do they notice about all the multiples of 10? What does this mean?

Page 4

Looking for Patterns

- Children need to have completed, and understood, The Language of Maths activity on page 2 and the Looking for Patterns activity on page 3 before starting on this activity.
- This game reinforces children's ability to count on in steps of five and recognise the multiples of five.
- Ensure children are familiar with the rules of the game before setting them off to play it independently. You may wish to spend a few minutes playing the game with the children to get them started.
- Children play variations of the game, for example, putting a counter on all the multiples of 10, 3 or 4.

AfL

- How would you describe the pattern of counters on this rectangle? What is the number sentence? What is the other number sentence that goes with this pattern?
- How did you work out the answer to the problem?
- What does the word 'multiple' mean?
- Tell me a multiple of 2 / 5 / 10.
- How do you know that a number is a multiple of 2 / 5 / 10?
- Can you tell me a multiple of 3 or 4?
- What is the next number in this pattern? What is the rule for this pattern? Can you tell me a number that would come before this first number in the pattern?
- Look at your number square. What do you notice about the number 10? What about all the other multiples of 10? What does this mean?
- How could you change this game to make it trickier?

Answers

Page 1

Let's Investigate
Results of the investigation will vary.

What's the Problem?
Mrs. Giles gets 35 eggs a week.
One hen lays 25 eggs in 5 weeks.
After Mrs Giles buys four more hens she will get 55 eggs a week.

Page 2

The Language of Maths
2, 4, 6, 8, 10, 12, 14, 16, 18, 20
5, 10, 15, 20, 25, 30, 35, 40, 45, 50
10, 20, 30, 40, 50, 60, 70, 80, 90, 100

3, 6, 9, 12, 15, 18
4, 8, 12, 16, 20, 24

What's the Problem?
There are 34 legs in the farmyard.

Page 3

Looking for Patterns
2, 4, 6, 8, **10**, **12**, **14**
9, 12, 15, 18, **21**, **24**, **27**
45, 40, 35, 30, **25**, **20**, **15**
20, 30, **40**, 50, **60**, **70**, 80
27, 25, 23, **21**, **19**, **17**, 15

Looking for Patterns

1	2	3	4	5	6	7	8	9	10
11	12	13	14	15	16	17	18	19	20
21	22	23	24	25	26	27	28	29	30
31	32	33	34	35	36	37	38	39	40
41	42	43	44	45	46	47	48	49	50
51	52	53	54	55	56	57	58	59	60
61	62	63	64	65	66	67	68	69	70
71	72	73	74	75	76	77	78	79	80
81	82	83	84	85	86	87	88	89	90
91	92	93	94	95	96	97	98	99	100

Page 4

Looking for Patterns
No answers required.

Inquisitive ant

multiple
A number that can be divided exactly by another smaller number without a remainder.

Prerequisites for learning

- Describe simple patterns and relationships involving numbers
- Solve a puzzle or problem in the context of money
- Count on or back in ones, twos, fives and tens and use this knowledge to derive the multiples of 2, 5 and 10
- Represent sharing and repeated subtraction (grouping) as division
- Use concrete objects, pictorial representations, arrays and related vocabulary to support division
- Understand the concept of 'some left over' (remainders) when dividing
- Understand that division is the inverse of multiplication and vice versa

Resources

pencil and paper

Resource sheet 2: My notes (optional)

Resource sheet 3: Pupil self assessment booklet (optional)

Resource sheet 7: Bookshelf

scissors

1, 2, 3 and 4 digit cards (optional)

Compare Bears (or similar)

counters

5p, 10p, 20p, 50p, £1 and £2 coins

Teaching support

Page 1

What's the Problem?

- Provide the children with 12 counters to represent the biscuits and Compare Bears to represent the different characters in the problems.
- What if the biscuits were shared between six people, how many will they each get?
- What if the biscuits were shared between Jake, Lisa and their mum and their dad, how many will they each get? Do the children realise that this is the same answer as when Jake and Lisa each invite a friend over to play and they share the biscuits between all four?

Page 2

Let's Investigate

- This activity reinforces children's understanding of division as sharing.
- As the children share the toys between the shelves, ask them to write what they have done.
- If appropriate, ask the children to write number sentences using the symbols ÷ and =.

What's the Problem?

- The first part of this activity reinforces children's understanding of division as grouping.
- If children have completed the previous activity (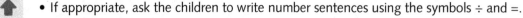 Let's Investigate), and the What's the Problem? activity on page 1, you may wish to discuss with them the similarities between these three activities – they each involve dividing 12 into equal sized groups. Can the children use what they discovered in the previous activities to help them with the second part of this activity?

Page 3

Let's Investigate

- The last two questions in this activity, i.e. 33 frogs and 37 frogs, reinforce children's understanding of rounding up after division.
- Ensure children do not spend too much time drawing elaborate lily pads.
- If children experience difficulty with the last two questions, get them to draw the frogs on each of the lily pads.

Money Matters

- If necessary, complete one of the questions with the children – counting on in multiples of the smaller coin until you reach the larger coin, e.g. How many 10p coins make 50p? 10, 20, 30, 40, 50. Five 10p coins make 50p.
- Provide the children with 5p, 10p, 20p, 50p, £1 and £2 coins.
- Ask the children to write similar statements comparing the values of two coins, e.g. ten 20p coins make a £2 coin; two 10p coins make a 20p coin.
- Ask the children to write similar statements comparing the values of coins and notes, e.g. five £1 coins make a £5 note; two £5 notes make a £10 note.

Page 4

Let's Investigate

- Provide the children with 1, 2, 3 and 4 digit cards.
- Ask the children what they notice about which numbers can be divided exactly by 2, 3 and 4. Discuss with them the link between their answers to this activity and the multiples of 2, 3 and 4.

What's the Problem?

- This activity reinforces children's understanding of division as grouping. It also involves division calculations with remainders. Ensure that the children are familiar with both these concepts before attempting this activity.
- This activity is easier if children realise that the number of CDs that Lisa has is somewhere in the range of 13 to 19 (inclusive) – the first clue tells them this.

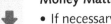

- What could you do to share out the biscuits fairly?
- How many toys are there on 2 / 3 / 4 shelves? Can you explain this to me as a number sentence?
- How did you work out the answer to this problem? Did you think of a number sentence? What was it?
- Did you use anything to help you work out the answer? How did this help?
- How many 20p coins are there in one pound? What about in two pounds?
- Take two coins and describe to me how many times one of the coins is larger / smaller than the other coin.
- What does it mean if a number can be divided exactly by two?

Answers

Page 1

What's the Problem?
4 biscuits.
6 biscuits.
3 biscuits.

Page 2

Let's Investigate
Putting all the toys onto 2 shelves: 6 toys per shelf.
Putting all the toys onto 3 shelves: 4 toys per shelf.
Putting all the toys onto 4 shelves: 3 toys per shelf.

What's the Problem?
There are 6 groups of 2 bears. The bears could also travel in:
- 4 groups of 3 bears
- 3 groups of 4 bears
- 2 groups of 6 bears

Page 3

Let's Investigate
Number of lily pads needed are:
15 frogs: 3 lily pads
25 frogs: 5 lily pads
33 frogs: 7 lily pads
37 frogs: 8 lily pads

Money Matters
$5 \times 10p = 50p$
$5 \times 20p = £1$
$4 \times 5p = 20p$
$4 \times 50p = £2$
$5 \times 2p = 10p$
$10 \times 10p = £1$

Page 4

Let's Investigate
The 12 different two-digit numbers are:
12, 13, 14, 21, 23, 24, 31, 32, 34, 41, 42 and 43
Numbers that can be divided exactly by 2:
12, 14, 24, 32, 34 and 42.
Numbers that can be divided exactly by 3:
12, 21, 24 and 42.
Numbers that can be divided exactly by 4:
12, 24 and 32.

What's the Problem?
Lisa has 17 CDs.

Inquisitive ant  ÷

The symbol for division.

Issue 12

Division

Prerequisites for learning

- Describe simple patterns and relationships involving numbers
- Solve a puzzle or problem in the context of money
- Recognise odd and even numbers
- Understand that halving is the inverse of doubling and derive and recall doubles of all numbers to 20, and the corresponding halves
- Count on or back in ones, twos, fives and tens and use this knowledge to derive the multiples of 2, 5 and 10
- Represent sharing and repeated subtraction (grouping) as division
- Use concrete objects, pictorial representations, arrays and related vocabulary to support division
- Understand that division is the inverse of multiplication and vice versa
- Understand and use the basic functions of a calculator

Resources

pencil and paper

Resource sheet 2: My notes (optional)

Resource sheet 3: Pupil self assessment booklet (optional)

interlocking cubes

calculator

counters

pencil and paper clip (for the spinner)

buttons (or similar)

Teaching support

Page 1

Let's Investigate

- As the children split the 16 cubes into towers all the same height, ask them to write what they have done.
- If appropriate, ask the children to write number sentences using the symbols ÷ and =.

Money Matters

- If children have completed the previous activity (Let's Investigate), you may wish to discuss with them the similarities between these two activities – they both involve dividing 20 into equal sized groups. Can the children use what they discovered in the previous activity to help them with this activity?

Page 2

Let's Investigate

- Ensure children understand what they are required to do in this activity. If necessary, choose an even number less than 50 (not 16, 20 or 40) and work with the children to keep halving the number until you reach an odd number.
- Referring to the three examples in the Issue, also ensure that the children understand why 16 is the longest of these number chains.

- Children start with any two-digit even number.

Looking for Patterns

- Allow the children to use a calculator.

- Once the children have completed this activity, arrange them into pairs or groups and ask them to discuss what patterns they noticed.

- Discuss with the children the rule for dividing a multiple of 10 by 10.

Page 3

Let's Investigate

- This highly practical activity reinforces children's understanding of division calculations with remainders.
- There are two parts to this activity. Firstly, investigating which numbers between 10 and 30 have remainders when divided by two, and secondly looking at the results of the investigation to identify patterns and make a generalisation.
- It is recommended that children have completed this activity before starting on the following activity (The Language of Maths).

- Children choose numbers between 10 and 50.

The Language of Maths

- It is recommended that children have completed the previous activity (Let's Investigate) before starting on this activity.

- Once the children have completed this activity, provide an opportunity for individual or pairs of children to share and discuss their definitions.

Page 4

The Language of Maths

- It is recommended that you play the game with the children before they play it by themselves. Also ensure that the children are familiar with how to use the spinner.

- As the children take turns to play the game, encourage them to say the related division calculation, e.g. 12 divided by 3 is 4.

What's the Problem?

- This activity is designed to provide an opportunity for children to demonstrate how they would work out the answer to a division calculation for which they do not have instant mental recall of the answer.

- If the calculation is too easy, ask the children to explain how they would work out the answer to another, more complicated division calculation, e.g. 96 ÷ 8, 63 ÷ 7 or 72 ÷ 12.

AfL

- How can you divide a rod of 16 interlocking cubes into towers all the same size?
- What was the largest number chain you could make? How could you make the number chain even longer? Think about doubling the first number.
- What happened when you divided each of these numbers by 10? What patterns do you notice?
- Tell me a number that when you divide it by 2 there is no remainder.
- Tell me a number that when you divide it by 2 there is a remainder of 1.
- How can you tell if a number will have a remainder when it is divided by 2? What do we call these numbers?
- What was a good number to spin when you were playing the game? What number did you not want to spin? Why?
- How did you work out the answer to this number sentence? Did you use anything to help you? How else might you work it out?

Answers

Page 1

Let's Investigate

16 interlocking cubes:
- 1 tower of 16 cubes
- 2 towers of 8 cubes
- 4 towers of 4 cubes
- 8 towers of 2 cubes
- 16 towers of 1 cube

20 interlocking cubes:
- 1 tower of 20 cubes
- 2 towers of 10 cubes
- 4 towers of 5 cubes
- 5 towers of 4 cubes
- 10 towers of 2 cubes
- 20 towers of 1 cube

24 interlocking cubes:
- 1 tower of 24 cubes
- 2 towers of 12 cubes
- 3 towers of 8 cubes
- 4 towers of 6 cubes
- 6 towers of 4 cubes
- 8 towers of 3 cubes
- 12 towers of 2 cubes
- 24 towers of 1 cube

Money Matters

2 friends would each receive £10.
4 friends would each receive £5.
5 friends would each receive £4.
10 friends would each receive £2.
20 friends would each receive £1.

Page 2

Let's Investigate

The longest number chain possible is 32:
$32 \rightarrow 16 \rightarrow 8 \rightarrow 4 \rightarrow 2 \rightarrow 1$

Looking for Patterns

$40 \div 10 = 4$
$50 \div 10 = 5$
$80 \div 10 = 8$
$30 \div 10 = 3$
$90 \div 10 = 9$
$60 \div 10 = 6$

Explanations will vary.

Page 3

Let's Investigate

The following numbers between 10 and 30 have a counter in the bin, i.e. a remainder of 1: 11, 13, 15, 17, 19, 21, 23, 25, 27 and 29.

The following numbers between 10 and 30 do not have a counter in the bin, i.e. no remainder: 12, 14, 16, 18, 20, 22, 24, 26 and 28.

Explanations will vary. However, they should describe how numbers with a counter in the bin (a remainder of 1) are all odd numbers and numbers without a counter in the bin (no remainders) are all even numbers.

The Language of Maths

Explanations will vary. However, in the context of division, the word 'remainder' refers to the amount left over when a number or quantity cannot be divided exactly by another number.

Page 4

The Language of Maths

No answer required.

What's the Problem?

Explanations will vary.

Inquisitive ant  sharing equally
Dividing a number, quantity or object into equal groups or pieces.

Mixed operations

Prerequisites for learning

- Describe simple patterns and relationships involving numbers
- Solve a puzzle or problem in the context of money
- Derive and recall all addition number bonds and related subtraction facts within 20
- Count on or back in ones, twos, fives and tens
- Solve practical problems that involve combining groups of 2, 5 or 10
- Use knowledge of number facts and operations to estimate and check answers to calculations
- Understand subtraction as 'take away' and find a 'difference' by counting up
- Understand that subtraction is the inverse of addition and vice versa and use this to derive and record related addition and subtraction number sentences
- Use concrete objects and pictorial representations to support the addition of a one-digit number or a multiple of 10 to a one-digit or two-digit number
- Add more than two numbers
- Read, write and interpret mathematical statements involving addition (+), subtraction (−) and equals (=) signs

Resources

pencil and paper

Resource sheet 2: My notes (optional)

Resource sheet 3: Pupil self assessment booklet (optional)

5p, 10p and 20p coins (optional)

set of 0–9 digit cards (optional)

Teaching support

Page 1

Looking for Patterns

- Before starting this activity, ensure the children realise that a calculation can involve more than two numbers and one operation, e.g. $6 + 2 - 4 = 4$.
- When the children have completed the activity, ask them to see what other answers they can get by changing the operations in each of the given calculations.
  For example, $5 + 2 + 3 = 10$ can become:
  $5 + 2 - 3 = 4$
  $5 - 2 + 3 = 6$
  $5 - 2 - 3 = 0$
- Can the children use the multiplication symbol as well as the addition and subtraction symbols?

Money Matters

- Ensure children realise that they can only use the eight 5p coins, six 10p coins and six 20p coins to make 40p. Also ensure they realise that they can use combinations of all three types of coins to make 40p.
- Encourage the children to write number sentences for each of their combinations of coins, either as addition calculations, e.g. $10p + 10p + 10p + 5p + 5p = 40p$, or multiplication and addition calculations, e.g. $3 \times 10p + 2 \times 5p = 40p$. If appropriate, you may also wish to introduce the use of brackets, i.e. $(3 \times 10p) + (2 \times 5p) = 40p$.
- Provide the children with 5p, 10p and 20p coins.

Page 2

The Puzzler

- Ensure the children understand the meaning of the terms 'sum' and 'difference'.
- Explain to the children that, not including the example, each of the numbers 1 to 10 are used only once in the five questions in this activity.
- Arrange the children into pairs and provide each pair with a set of 0–9 digit cards. Children shuffle the cards and spread them out face down on the table. They take turns to choose two of the cards, e.g. 5 and 7 (not showing them to their partner), and work out the sum and difference between the two numbers. They then tell their partner these two answers, e.g. *The sum of my two numbers is 12. The difference between my two numbers is 2.* Can their partner guess which two cards they chose? The child who chose the cards shows them to their partner to check.

Let's Investigate

- This activity introduces children to two very important laws of arithmetic. Firstly, the commutative law as it applies to addition, i.e. 2 + 6 = 6 + 2, and how it is more effective and efficient to answer an addition calculation by putting the larger number first and adding on the smaller number. Secondly, it also demonstrates the inverse relationship between addition and subtraction.

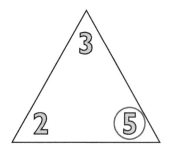

- Ensure the children realise that for each 'trio', the larger number is the answer to the two addition calculations, as well as being the first number (the minuend) in each of the subtraction calculations. If necessary, tell the children to circle the larger number in each of the 'trios' before they start to write the four number sentences.
- Children need to have completed this activity before starting on the Let's Investigate activity on page 3.
- It is also recommended that children have completed this activity before starting on the Looking for Patterns activity on page 2 of Issue 14 – Mixed operations.

Page 3

Let's Investigate

- Children need to have completed the Let's Investigate activity on page 2 before starting on this activity.
- It is also recommended that children have completed this activity before starting on the Looking for Patterns activity on page 2 of Issue 14 – Mixed operations.
- You may wish to ask the children to work in pairs to do this activity.
- Once individuals or pairs have completed this activity, arrange them into pairs or groups to compare and discuss their 'trios'.
- Suggest the children write 'trios' for some of the addition and subtraction number facts to 5.
- Encourage the children to write 'trios' for some of the addition and subtraction number facts to 20.

The Puzzler

- Suggest the children begin by working out the solution to the second question,

i.e.  = 15p.

Once they know that one pencil costs 5p, they can use this to work out the solution to the first question and then the final question.

Page 4

Around the World

- Begin this activity by 'walking' a route from Lisa's home to the shops to demonstrate to the children what is involved in this activity.
- If appropriate, encourage the children to write down the number sentence for each of the different totals.
- Ask children to investigate the smallest and largest totals they can make.

AfL

- How did you know that an addition / subtraction sign needed to go here?
- Tell me one of the ways you made 40p. Can you make 40p using 3 / 4 / 5 coins?
- Tell me two numbers that have a sum of 10 and a difference of 4.
- What relationships do you notice between these numbers?
- If 4 + 6 = 10 what other addition number sentence do you know that uses the same three numbers? What subtraction number sentence do you know? Can you tell me another subtraction number sentence that uses the same three numbers?
- Can you tell me three other numbers that have the same special relationship where you can make two addition and two subtraction number sentences?
- How did you work out the answer to this problem? What is the number sentence?
- What are the different totals you made? What is the largest / smallest total you can make?

Answers

Page 1

Looking for Patterns

5 + 2 + 3 = 10	9 + 3 − 2 = 10
3 − 2 + 1 = 2	6 − 3 − 2 = 1
7 − 5 + 2 = 4	8 + 2 − 5 = 5

Money Matters

20p, 20p	20p, 10p, 10p
20p, 10p, 5p, 5p	20p, 5p, 5p, 5p, 5p
10p, 10p, 10p, 10p	10p, 10p, 10p, 5p, 5p
10p, 10p, 5p, 5p, 5p	10p, 5p, 5p, 5p, 5p, 5p, 5p
5p, 5p, 5p, 5p, 5p, 5p, 5p, 5p	

Page 2

The Puzzler

2 and 4 have a sum of 6 and a difference of 2.
3 and 7 have a sum of 10 and a difference of 4.
1 and 8 have a sum of 9 and a difference of 7.
6 and 9 have a sum of 15 and a difference of 3.
5 and 10 have a sum of 15 and a difference of 5.

Let's Investigate

2 + 3 = 5	5 + 4 = 9	4 + 2 = 6	7 + 3 = 10
3 + 2 = 5	4 + 5 = 9	2 + 4 = 6	3 + 7 = 10
5 − 3 = 2	9 − 4 = 5	6 − 2 = 4	10 − 3 = 7
5 − 2 = 3	9 − 5 = 4	6 − 4 = 2	10 − 7 = 3

Page 3

Let's Investigate
Results of the investigation will vary.

The Puzzler
A pencil costs 5p.
A sharpener costs 20p.
A ruler costs 50p.
A ruler and a pencil cost 55p.

Page 4

Around the World
Totals will vary.

Inquisitive ant

sum
The whole of something. A word used to describe addition.

Mixed operations

Prerequisites for learning

- Describe simple patterns and relationships involving numbers
- Solve a puzzle or problem in the context of money
- Derive and recall all addition number bonds and related subtraction facts within 20
- Count on or back in ones, twos, fives and tens and use this knowledge to derive the multiples of 2, 5 and 10
- Solve practical problems that involve combining groups of 2, 5 or 10
- Use knowledge of number facts and operations to estimate and check answers to calculations
- Use concrete objects and pictorial representations to support the addition of a one-digit number or a multiple of 10 to a one-digit or two-digit number
- Add more than two numbers
- Read, write and interpret mathematical statements involving addition (+), subtraction (−) and equals (=) signs

Resources

pencil and paper

Resource sheet 2: My notes (optional)

Resource sheet 3: Pupil self assessment booklet (optional)

1–6 dice

counters

coloured pencils (optional)

0–9 dice (optional)

Teaching support

Page 1

The Puzzler

- Tell the children that there is more than one possible route through the maze. Can they find them? Suggest they use a different coloured pencil to draw in the different route(s).

Page 2

Looking for Patterns

- This activity reinforces children's understanding of two very important laws of arithmetic. Firstly, the commutative law as it applies to addition, i.e. 2 + 6 = 6 + 2, and how it is more effective and efficient to answer an addition calculation by putting the larger number first and adding on the smaller number. Secondly, it also demonstrates the inverse relationship between addition and subtraction.
- If the children have already completed the 🐝 Let's Investigate activities on pages 2 and 3 in Issue 13 – Mixed operations, then they should be quicker at identifying the missing numbers in this activity.
- Once the children have finished this activity, discuss with them the similarities between this activity and the two activities in Issue 13 referred to above.

The Puzzler

- This activity introduces children, in an extremely informal way, to the concept of algebra as substitution.
- Children need to have completed this activity before starting 🐝 The Puzzler activity on page 3.

- When the children have completed this activity suggest they substitute other numbers for each of the letters A to F. However, it is important that before they do this they understand the need to make the first letter in each of the subtraction calculations the larger number. They also need to think carefully about the division calculation. When the children have done this they then give these new numbers to a friend to use to answer the nine problems.

Page 3

Money Matters

- There is more than one solution to the second and third of these problems. Therefore once the children have finished this activity, arrange them into pairs or groups and ask them to compare and discuss their solutions. How are they different? How are they the same?

The Puzzler

- Children need to have completed The Puzzler activity on page 2 before starting this activity.
- Children write other calculations using the numbers in 🐜 The Puzzler activity on page 2, e.g. 10 + 7 − 3 = 14. They then rewrite each of the calculations omitting the numbers to the left of the equals sign, i.e. ☐ + ☐ − ☐ = 14, and give them to a friend to solve. When their friend has answered all the questions, they compare calculations.

Page 4

The Puzzler

- This activity consolidates children's recall of the addition number facts for each number to at least 10, as well as pairs of numbers that total 20.
- As the children take turns in playing the game, encourage them to say the related addition and subtraction number facts.
- Children play the game with two 0–9 dice.

AfL

- There is more than one way to reach a total of four through this maze. Can you find me another way?
- How did you know that the number 5 belonged here?
- What is special about these three numbers?
- How did you work out the answer to this question? What are the numbers that belong here?
- How did you begin to solve this puzzle?
- Can you make up another number sentence using these letters? Write down the sign and the answer. Let's see if I can work out what the numbers should be.
- What is the difference between 8 and 20? What do you have to do to get the answer?
- Tell me two numbers that make 20.

Answers

Page 1

The Puzzler
Other routes are possible.

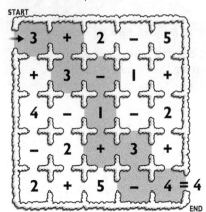

Page 2

Looking for Patterns

1 + 4 = 5	3 + 7 = 10	2 + 6 = 8
4 + 1 = 5	7 + 3 = 10	6 + 2 = 8
5 − 4 = 1	10 − 7 = 3	8 − 6 = 2
5 − 1 = 4	10 − 3 = 7	8 − 2 = 6

The Puzzler

A + F = 11   E − C = 2   B + C + D = 21

B − F = 3   A − F = 5   C lots of D is 50

D + E = 17   D shared between C is 2   E + F − D = 0

Page 3

Money Matters

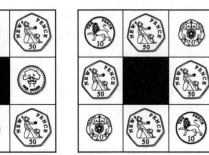
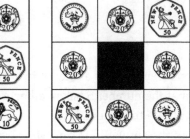

Other solutions are possible.

The Puzzler

D + B = 16
or
A + A = 16

E − F = 4
or
D − B = 4

A + C + E = 20
or
D + C + C = 20
or
D + E + F = 20
or
A + B + B = 20
or
E + E + B = 20

E + C = 12
or
B + B = 12

B lots of C is 30
or
D lots of F is 30

B shared between F is 2
or
D shared between C is 2

Page 4

The Puzzler
No answer required.

Inquisitive ant

total
The result of one or more additions.

Mixed operations

Prerequisites for learning

- Describe simple patterns and relationships involving numbers
- Solve a puzzle or problem in the context of money
- Derive and recall all addition number bonds and related subtraction facts within 20
- Use knowledge of number facts and operations to estimate and check answers to calculations
- Use concrete objects and pictorial representations to support the addition of a one-digit number or a multiple of 10 to a one-digit or two-digit number
- Add more than two numbers
- Read, write and interpret mathematical statements involving addition (+), subtraction (−) and equals (=) signs

Resources

pencil and paper
Resource sheet 2: My notes (optional)
Resource sheet 3: Pupil self assessment booklet (optional)
calculator

Teaching support

Page 1

Technology Today

- Ensure children are familiar with, and are able to confidently use, a calculator before setting them off to work independently on this activity.
- If necessary, discuss with the children the different calculations that are possible, e.g. addition of two numbers, addition of more than two numbers, subtraction, multiplication and, if appropriate, division. You may also wish to discuss with the children how the digits can be arranged to form two-digit or even three-digit numbers, e.g. 12 + 43; 132 − 4.
- What if the keys the children were able to use were 2, 3, 4 and 5?

Let's Investigate

- Ensure children realise that a dart can hit the same number twice in a calculation, e.g. 14 = 10 + 2 + 2.
- Finding a solution to the numbers 18 and 19 are the ones that children may have most difficulty with.
- Once children have completed the activity, arrange them into pairs to compare and discuss their calculations.
- Ask the children to see if they can make all the numbers from 1 to 30 or 40.

Page 2

Money Matters

- Ensure the children realise that the lines do not need to be straight lines.
- What is the smallest total possible joining four coins? What is the largest total possible joining four coins?

Let's Investigate

- Emphasise to the children that they can only use each number once in each number sentence.
- Encourage the children to use multiplication and division, as well as addition and subtraction, e.g. $2 \times 5 = 10$ and $4 \times 5 \div 2 = 10$. If appropriate, you may wish to introduce the use of brackets, i.e. $(4 \times 5) \div 2 = 10$.

Page 3

Looking for Patterns

- What are all the different ways of putting six counters into three boxes? (If necessary, tell the children that there are 10 different ways.)

Page 4

Money Matters

- Ensure children fully understand this activity and what is happening in each of the moneyboxes.
- When the children have completed this activity, discuss with them the strategies they used for working out how much money was left inside each moneybox.

AfL

- Tell me a number sentence that uses 1, 2, 3 or 4. What is the answer?
- What is the largest answer you can get using only the digits 1, 2, 3 and 4 in the number sentence?
- How did you make the number 8 / 13 / 17... using only the numbers 1, 2, 5 and 10?
- Can you tell me how you might make a number larger than 20 using only the numbers 1, 2, 5 and 10?
- What was the smallest / largest total you could make joining three coins together? What if you joined four coins together?
- Can you write a number sentence with an answer of 10 that uses the times / multiplication sign?
- Tell me one of the ways you can divide five counters between three boxes.
- Tell me how you worked out how much money was left inside this moneybox.

Answers

Page 1

Technology Today
Calculations will vary.

Let's Investigate

1 = 1	2 = 2
3 = 2 + 1	4 = 2 + 2
5 = 5	6 = 5 + 1
7 = 5 + 2	8 = 5 + 2 + 1
9 = 5 + 2 + 2	10 = 10
11 = 10 + 1	12 = 10 + 2
13 = 10 + 2 + 1	14 = 10 + 2 + 2
15 = 10 + 5	16 = 10 + 5 + 1
17 = 10 + 5 + 2	18 = 10 + 5 + 2 + 1
19 = 10 + 5 + 2 + 2	20 = 10 + 10

Page 2

Money Matters
Totals will vary.
The smallest possible total is 4p.
The largest possible total is 25p.

Let's Investigate
Results of the investigation will vary.

Page 3

Looking for Patterns
The 6 different ways of putting 5 counters into 3 boxes are:

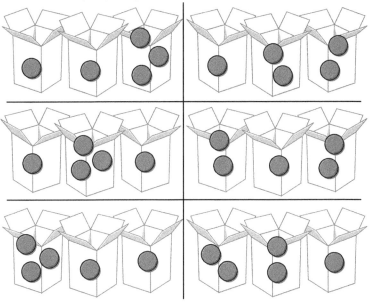

Page 4

Money Matters
55p   60p   £4   £1.50

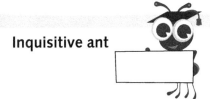

Inquisitive ant

<   The symbol for 'is less than'.

Mixed operations

Prerequisites for learning

- Describe simple patterns and relationships involving numbers
- Solve a puzzle or problem in the context of money
- Derive and recall all addition number bonds and related subtraction facts within 20
- Understand that halving is the inverse of doubling and derive and recall doubles of all numbers to 20, and the corresponding halves
- Count on or back in ones, twos, fives and tens and use this knowledge to derive the multiples of 2, 5 and 10
- Solve practical problems that involve combining groups of 2, 5 or 10
- Use knowledge of number facts and operations to estimate and check answers to calculations
- Use concrete objects and pictorial representations to support the addition of a one-digit number or a multiple of 10 to a one-digit or two-digit number
- Add more than two numbers
- Use concrete objects and pictorial representations to support the subtraction of a one-digit number from a one-digit or two-digit number and a multiple of 10 from a two-digit number
- Read, write and interpret mathematical statements involving addition (+), subtraction (−) and equals (=) signs

Resources

pencil and paper

Resource sheet 2: My notes (optional)

Resource sheet 3: Pupil self assessment booklet (optional)

1p, 2p, 5p, 10p, 20p, 50p and £1 coins (optional)

set of 0–9 digit cards and the +, −, and = operator cards (optional)

ten 1p coins, five 2p coins and five 10p coins

scissors

glue

Teaching support

Page 1

Let's Investigate

- You may wish to tell the children a particular number to write on their engine, e.g. 10 or 20.
- Encourage the children to write addition, subtraction, and if appropriate, multiplication and division number sentences for their chosen number. Also remind the children that they are able to write calculations that involve more than two numbers and one operation, for example 8 + 7 − 3 = 12.

Page 2

Money Matters

- Encourage the children to record their results as addition number sentences.
- Provide the children with a 5p, 10p, 20p and 50p coin.
- Tell the children that there are four different amounts possible (including the one given in the Issue).

Let's Investigate

- Ensure the children realise that each of the digits in a one-digit or two-digit number, as well as the addition, subtraction and equals symbols all constitute the five, six or seven cards used to make each number sentence.
- Other calculations using five cards are:
  $2 + 3 = 5$
  $9 - 4 = 5, 8 - 3 = 5, 7 - 2 = 5, 6 - 1 = 5$
- Other calculations using six cards are:
  $12 - 7 = 5, 13 - 8 = 5, 14 - 9 = 5$
- There are many possible calculations using seven cards involving subtraction.
- Provide the children with a set of 0–9 digit cards and the +, −, and = operator cards.
- Ask the children to make number sentences using eight cards where the answer is 5, e.g. $14 - 7 - 2 = 5$.
- Ask the children to use the multiplication and division symbols, e.g. $5 \times 4 = 20$, $10 \div 2 = 5$.

Page 3

Money Matters

- Ensure children realise that for each row of coins they are required to work out two calculations. The first is finding the total of the coins shown in the row. The second is finding the total of the coins after several coins in the row have been replaced by a different coin.
- Provide the children with a selection of coins to use.
- Once the children have completed the activity, arrange them into pairs or groups and discuss with them the various strategies they used for working out the different totals. In particular, focus on the second calculation the children did for each row of coins. Did they recognise any patterns that helped them work out these answers?

Page 4

The Puzzler

- Once the children have played the game several times, discuss with them the strategies for winning the game. Ask for the children's ideas as to what amounts are good to choose to place on the hand at different stages in the game.
- Children play the game choosing 1p, 2p or 3p when it's their turn. Discuss with them how the strategies for winning the game are different from those when playing the game choosing either 1p or 2p each turn.
- Children play the game as described in the Issue in groups of three. Discuss with them how the strategies for winning the game are different from those when playing the game in pairs.

AfL

- What is your favourite number? Tell me a number sentence that has as its answer the number ….
- What is the smallest / largest amount of money you can have using only three of these coins?
- Tell me some of the number sentences you were able to make that had an answer of 5. Which do you think was the cleverest number sentence? Why do you think it is this one?
- What was the total of this row of coins before the coins were changed? What was the total after they were changed? Was this more or less?
- How did you work out the total of this row of coins? How did counting in steps of 2 help you?
- Was there a clever way to play the game? What was it?

Answers

Page 1

Let's Investigate
Results of the investigation will vary.

Page 2

Money Matters
5p + 10p + 20p = 35p
5p + 10p + 50p = 65p
10p + 20p + 50p = 80p
5p + 20p + 50p = 75p

Let's Investigate
Number sentences will vary.

Page 3

Money Matters
Before: 50p   After: 70p
Before: 12p   After: 9p
Before: £5   After: £4
Before: 9p   After: 12p
Before: £1   After: 80p

Page 4

The Puzzler
No answer required.

Inquisitive ant

altogether
The total quantity or number. A word most commonly associated with addition.

Mixed operations

Prerequisites for learning

- Describe simple patterns and relationships involving numbers
- Solve a puzzle or problem in the context of money
- Derive and recall all addition number bonds and related subtraction facts within 20
- Understand that halving is the inverse of doubling and derive and recall doubles of all numbers to 20, and the corresponding halves
- Count on or back in ones, twos, fives and tens and use this knowledge to derive the multiples of 2, 5 and 10
- Solve practical problems that involve combining groups of 2, 5 or 10
- Use knowledge of number facts and operations to estimate and check answers to calculations
- Add more than two numbers
- Understand that subtraction is the inverse of addition and vice versa and use this to derive and record related addition and subtraction number sentences
- Use concrete objects, pictorial representations, arrays and related vocabulary to support multiplication and division
- Read, write and interpret mathematical statements involving addition (+), subtraction (–) and equals (=) signs

Resources

pencil and paper

Resource sheet 2: My notes (optional)

Resource sheet 3: Pupil self assessment booklet (optional)

Resource sheet 6: Dogs, cats and chickens

scissors

glue

large sheet of paper

six 1–6 dice

counters

Teaching support

Page 1

Money Matters

- Ensure the children have worked out that there is a total of £12 on the table.

- Tell the children that Susan had a total of seven coins in her money box. Which coins might she have had?

Looking for Patterns

- For this activity, children require only the bottom section of Resource sheet 6 : Dogs, cats and chickens.
- This highly practical activity consolidates children's understanding of pairs and trios of numbers that total 12.

- Ask children to make pairs and trios of animals that total 14, 16 and 20.

Page 2

Let's Investigate

- Begin this activity by taking a route from Enter to Exit to demonstrate to the children what is involved in this activity.
- If appropriate, encourage the children to write down the number sentence for each of the amounts of gold coins they collect.
- Ask children to investigate the smallest and largest number of gold coins they can collect as they move through the house.

Page 3

Looking for Patterns

- This activity consolidates children's recall of pairs of numbers that total 10. It is also designed to provide an opportunity for children to demonstrate their different mental calculation strategies.
- Children need to have completed this activity before starting on the following 🐜 Looking for Patterns activity.

Looking for Patterns

- Children need to have completed the previous 🐜 Looking for Patterns activity before starting on this activity.
- Although the key mental calculation strategy is to look for pairs of numbers that total 10, add these two numbers together and then add the remaining numbers (preferably starting with the larger), some children may use equally effective and efficient strategies. Therefore it is recommended that once the children have completed this, and the previous activity, you arrange them into pairs or groups so that they can compare and discuss their methods.

Page 4

Looking for Patterns

- This activity reinforces children's understanding of the concepts of division as sharing and multiplication as repeated addition.
- Ensure children realise that they place the counters on the boxes at the top of the table and write the answer to the question 'How many counters is this altogether?' in the final column of the table, i.e. 'Total number of counters'.
- If necessary, work through the first part of this activity with the children and show them how to record the answers in the table (see Answers).
- Children continue putting counters in the boxes until there is a total of 40 counters.

AfL

- What coins might Susan / Ruby have had in her moneybox? Could she have had different coins to this?
- How many different groups of 12 animals were you able to make using two different animals? What about using three animals?
- Which way through the house gave you the most gold coins? Which way gave you the least gold coins?
- Why does arranging the numbers this way make it easier to add the numbers together? What are you looking to do when you move the numbers around?
- Look at your table. What patterns do you notice?
- What if you put two counters in each box each time?

Answers

Page 1

Money Matters
Susan's moneybox: any combination of coins that totals £7, e.g. 3 × £2 and £1 (other combinations are possible).
Ruby had £5 in her moneybox, e.g. 4 × £1 and 2 × 50p (other combinations are possible).

Looking for Patterns
12 animals made from two different animals. Many answers are possible including:
- 6 dogs and 6 chickens
- 8 dogs and 4 cats
- 10 chickens and 2 cats

12 animals made from three different animals. Many answers are possible including:
- 6 dogs, 4 cats and 2 chickens
- 5 dogs, 4 cats and 3 chickens
- 7 dogs, 3 cats and 2 chickens

Page 2

Let's Investigate
Results of the investigation will vary.

Page 3

Looking for Patterns
Explanations will vary. However, they should make mention of looking for pairs of numbers that total 10.

Looking for Patterns
Results of the investigation will vary.

Page 4

Looking for Patterns

	Box 1	Box 2	Box 3	Box 4	Total number of counters
4 counters	1 counter	1 counter	1 counter	1 counter	4
+ 4 more	2	2	2	2	8
+ 4 more	3	3	3	3	12
+ 4 more	4	4	4	4	16
+ 4 more	5	5	5	5	20

Inquisitive ant

=
The equals symbol, meaning 'the same as'.

Mixed operations

Prerequisites for learning

- Describe simple patterns and relationships involving numbers
- Solve a puzzle or problem in the context of money
- Derive and recall all addition and subtraction number bonds and related subtraction facts within 20
- Understand that halving is the inverse of doubling and derive and recall doubles of all numbers to 20, and the corresponding halves
- Count on or back in ones, twos, fives and tens and use this knowledge to derive the multiples of 2, 5 and 10
- Solve practical problems that involve combining groups of 2, 5 or 10
- Use knowledge of number facts and operations to estimate and check answers to calculations
- Use concrete objects and pictorial representations to support the addition of a one-digit number to a one-digit or two-digit number
- Add more than two numbers
- Use concrete objects and pictorial representations to support the subtraction of a one-digit number from a one-digit or two-digit number
- Understand that subtraction is the inverse of addition and vice versa and use this to derive and record related addition and subtraction number sentences
- Use concrete objects, pictorial representations, arrays and related vocabulary to support multiplication and division
- Read, write and interpret mathematical statements involving addition (+), subtraction (-) and equals (=) signs

Resources

pencil and paper

Resource sheet 2: My notes (optional)

Resource sheet 3: Pupil self assessment booklet (optional)

Resource sheet 6: Dogs, cats and chickens

Teaching support

Page 1

What's the Problem?

- Once the children have completed this activity, discuss with them how they worked out the answer to each of the three questions. Which question did they answer first? Did the answer to this question help them to work out the answers to the other two questions? If so, how?

Sports Update

- This question reinforces children's understanding of the inverse relationship between addition and subtraction.
- Ensure children are familiar with the terms: 'less than' and 'greater than'.
- If children are having difficulties, point out that any one of the last three clues will give them the answer – they do not have to work out all of them.

Page 2

The Puzzler

- Draw another ring around three numbers that total 12. Do the children realise that there are three possible solutions to this question?

Technology Today

- Allow the children to discover for themselves that they need to use the inverse operation from that written on the function machine to work out what number went into the machine.
- When the children have finished this activity you may wish to discuss with them the inverse relationship between addition and subtraction.

Page 3

Looking for Patterns

- For this activity, children require only the bottom section of Resource sheet 6: Dogs, cats and chickens.
- Children will not have enough chickens to make all the leg variations if they have the five chickens variation (See Answers). If appropriate, suggest they represent this variation using one chicken picture and writing the operation '× 5'.

Let's Investigate

- Children need to be confident in writing addition and subtraction calculations in order to successfully complete this activity.
- By referring to the example in the Issue, i.e. 3 + 2 = 5, ensure children realise that the answer to each calculation must be 2, 3, 5 or 10.

Page 4

Let's Investigate

- There are two parts to this activity. Firstly, writing number sentences that total 10. Secondly, using the number sentences for 10 to help write some number sentences that total 20.
- If necessary, discuss with the children how a number sentence for 10 can be used to help write a number sentence for 20, e.g. 6 + 4 = 10 ∴ 16 + 4 = 20 or 6 + 14 = 20.

- If appropriate, you may also wish to introduce to the children the use of brackets, e.g. (2 × 3) + 4 = 10.

AfL

- How did you work out the cost of 4 / 1 / 3 cones?
- How did you work out what Roshan's number was? Which clues told you straight away what her number was?
- How did you work out which number went into this function machine?
- What would come out of the machine if the number 7 went in instead of the number 4?
- How many different ways did you find to make a group of animals with 6 ears / 10 legs? Tell me one / two / three … of them. Are there any more ways?
- What are the eight number sentences that Kate was able to make?
- Tell me a number sentence that has an answer of 10. Does this help you work out a number sentence that has an answer of 20?
- If you know this number sentence, what other number sentences do you also know?

Answers

Page 1

What's the Problem?
4 cones cost £3.20.
1 cone costs 80p.
3 cones cost £2.40.

Sports Update
Roshan is number 24.

Page 2

The Puzzler

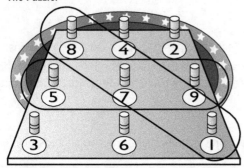

Other solutions are possible.

Technology Today

Page 3

Looking for Patterns
Ears
3 dogs
2 dogs, 1 cat
1 dog, 2 cats
3 cats

Legs
2 dogs, 1 chicken
1 dog, 3 chickens
1 dog, 1 cat, 1 chicken
1 cat, 3 chickens
2 cats, 1 chicken
5 chickens

Let's Investigate
Kate is right.

2 + 3 = 5	5 + 3 = 8
3 + 2 = 5	3 + 5 = 8
5 − 3 = 2	8 − 3 = 5
5 − 2 = 3	8 − 5 = 3

Page 4

Let's Investigate
Results of the investigation will vary.

Inquisitive ant  cost
The amount that has to be paid for something (the price).

Fractions

Prerequisites for learning

- Solve problems involving halving in the context of numbers
- Describe simple patterns and relationships involving numbers or shapes
- Use the vocabulary of halves and quarters in context
- Find one half and one quarter of an object, shape or quantity

Resources

pencil and paper

Resource sheet 2: My notes (optional)

Resource sheet 3: Pupil self assessment booklet (optional)

Resource sheet 8: Halves

coloured pencil

ruler

Teaching support

Page 1

Let's Investigate

- Tell the children that there are six different possible arrangements for both the square and the circle.
- You may wish to discuss with the children how the shapes in each of these sets are the same, just in different transformations.

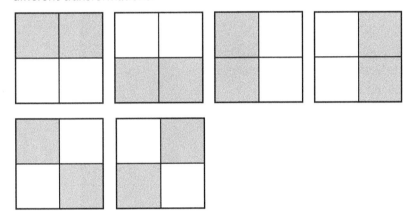

The Puzzler

- Encourage children to use a ruler when dividing the cake into the four equal parts.
- Ask the children if they can divide the cake into eight equal pieces of a different shape, using just four straight cuts.

Page 2

Looking for Patterns

- Tell the children that there are nine different possible arrangements – two of which are given.

What's the Problem?

- Ensure children realise that in order for there to be one quarter crabs, there needs to be a total of eight fish and crabs in the bucket. Therefore the children need to draw four more fish.

Page 3

Let's Investigate

- Ensure children realise that there is no one correct way to colour in half of any of these shapes, as long as the correct fraction has been coloured in.

- Once the children have completed the activity, arrange them into pairs or groups and ask them to discuss and compare their results.

The Puzzler

- This activity highlights the link between fractions and division.

- If necessary, discuss and demonstrate to the children the number of cuts that are required to divide a Strawberry Log into three pieces (thirds),i.e. two cuts.

- Once the children have completed the activity, discuss with them how, once the large Strawberry Log has been cut into five pieces, it has actually been divided into fifths. Extend this to talk about other unitary fractions, i.e. fractions with a numerator of 1.

Page 4

Focus on Science

- It is recommended that you suggest to the children that they begin this activity by counting how many of each insect / animal there is in the bug-tank, and writing this number in the respective section of the tank. Before children then circle the given fraction of each type of insect / animal, they can compare their totals with a friend.

AfL

- Show me some different ways to shade half of a square / circle.
- How did you work out the solution to this puzzle?
- Can you find any other ways of putting two halves together? How do you know that there are no other possible ways of doing this?
- What does one quarter mean?
- How else could you shade each of these shapes and still be right? Are there any other ways?
- What is half of 8? How does this activity show that?

Answers

Page 1

Let's Investigate

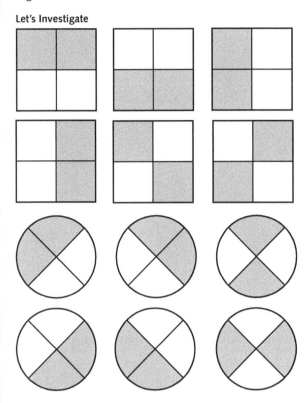

The Puzzler

Page 2

Looking for Patterns

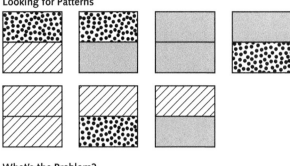

What's the Problem?

Half are fish.
In order that one quarter of all are crabs, the children need to draw four more fish.

Page 3

Let's Investigate

Answers will vary.

The Puzzler

Four cuts are needed to divide the log into five pieces.

Page 4

Focus on Science

Other solutions are possible.

Inquisitive ant

$\frac{1}{2}$ Symbol for half, meaning one part or group of something that is divided into two equal parts or groups.

Prerequisites for learning

- Solve problems involving halving in the context of numbers
- Describe simple patterns and relationships involving numbers or shapes
- Use the vocabulary of halves and quarters in context
- Find one half and one quarter of an object, shape or quantity
- Recognise and know the value of different denominations of coins and notes

Resources

pencil and paper

Resource sheet 2: My notes (optional)

Resource sheet 3: Pupil self assessment booklet (optional)

Resource sheet 9: Quarters

coloured pencils

A4 paper

interlocking cubes

Teaching support

Page 1

The Arts Roundup

- Ensure children understand that a ballerina can have a coloured tutu and be wearing a crown.

Construct

- You may wish to discuss with the children how each of these folded pieces of paper are the same, just in different transformations.

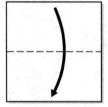  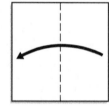 

Page 2

Let's Investigate

- Once the children have completed the activity, arrange them into pairs to compare and discuss their results.
- Ask the children to identify shapes that are the same, just in different transformations, e.g.

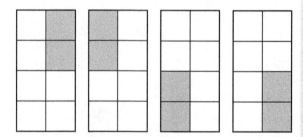

Let's Investigate

- Discuss with the children how the whole shape is made from:

  – sides, not corners, touching, i.e.

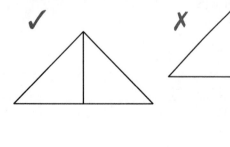

– complete sides touching, i.e.

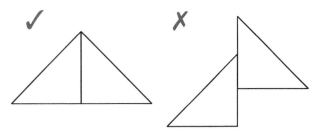

 • Tell the children that for each of the half shapes shown, it is possible that there is more than one whole shape. Can they find all the different whole shapes?

Page 3

The Puzzler

• If the children have previously answered The Puzzler activity on page 4 of Issue 22 – Length and height, you may like to discuss with them the similarities between the two activities.

 • Provide the children with interlocking cubes to make the rods.

• Children investigate halves and quarters of other lengths of rods using interlocking cubes.

The Puzzler

• Prior to setting the children off to work independently on this activity, discuss it with them, ensuring that they understand what is required.

• Ask the children to make trains of 4 or 8 cubes.

• Encourage the children to make trains of 12, 16 or 20 cubes.

Page 4

Money Matters

• Ensure the children are familiar with money and know the value of different denominators of coins.

• Ask the children to create a similar puzzle using 'quarter of' rather than 'half of' statements.

AfL

• What does this sign mean: $\frac{1}{2}$? What about $\frac{1}{4}$?

• If there is a one in the top number of a fraction, what does this mean? What does the bottom number of a fraction tell us?

• How many different ways could you fold a sheet of paper in quarters?

• Show me some different ways to shade a quarter of a rectangle / circle.

• How did you work out the solution to this puzzle / problem?

• How did you work out how many cubes Wilber would need to make a rod half / a quarter length?

• What did you do to work out the length of Wilber's second rod?

• Show me your 'train' of interlocking cubes. Put your train inside the tunnel so only one 'carriage' is showing. What fraction of your train is this?

• What was tricky about this activity? Was it easy to work out how many 'carriages' your partner's 'train' had? Why? Why not?

• How did you work out what half of 50p was?

Answers

Page 1

The Arts Roundup
Six ballerinas with yellow tutus, and three ballerinas wearing a crown.

Construct

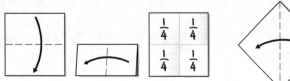

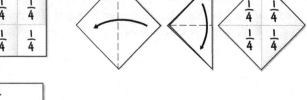

Page 2

Let's Investigate
Shadings will vary.

Let's Investigate

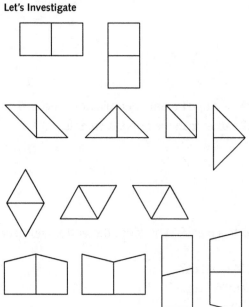

Page 3

The Puzzler
Wilber would need two cubes to make a rod half the length of his rod.

Wilber would need one cube to make a rod a quarter the length of his rod.

Wilber used 12 cubes to build his second rod.

The Puzzler
Results of the investigation will vary.

Page 4

Money Matters

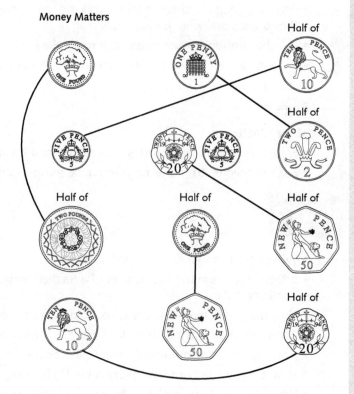

Inquisitive ant

$\frac{1}{4}$

Symbol for one quarter, meaning one part or group of something that is divided into four equal parts or groups.

Prerequisites for learning

- Solve problems involving halving in the context of numbers
- Describe simple patterns and relationships involving numbers or shapes
- Use the vocabulary of halves and quarters in context
- Find one half and one quarter of an object, shape or quantity
- Recognise and know the value of different denominations of coins and notes

Resources

pencil and paper
Resource sheet 2: My notes (optional)
Resource sheet 3: Pupil self assessment booklet (optional)
coloured pencils
counters
1–6 dice
£1 coins (optional)

Teaching support

Page 1

Let's Investigate

- If necessary, provide the children with counters (or similar) to help them with this activity. Referring to the example in the Issue, use the counters to demonstrate to the children that 3 is indeed one quarter of 12, i.e.

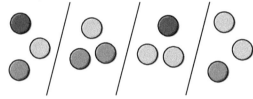

- Can the children use their results to work out what three quarters of a number is? For example, three quarters of 12 is 9, i.e.

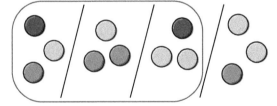

Money Matters

- Some children may need assistance in recording their results, e.g. $\frac{1}{2}$ of 2p is 1p.
- Ask the children to find a pair of coins where one coin is one-tenth of the other coin.

Page 2

The Puzzler

- What if Jack and Jill have eaten three quarters of their cherries? How many cherries have they each eaten? How many cherries did they each start with?

What's the Problem?

- If children are having difficulty working out one quarter of 16, tell them to divide the bees into groups of four and then cross out one bee from each group and count the remaining bees.

Page 3

The Puzzler

- If both Lee and Amy each ate half of their pizza, how many slices would they each eat? What if they each only ate one quarter of their pizza, how many slices would they each eat?

Money Matters

- Provide the children with £1 coins to help them work out the solutions to the two problems, e.g.

- What if $\frac{1}{4}$, $\frac{1}{3}$, $\frac{1}{5}$, $\frac{1}{6}$, ... $\frac{1}{10}$ of all the money that Jake had was £3?

  What if $\frac{1}{2}$, $\frac{1}{3}$, $\frac{1}{5}$, $\frac{1}{6}$, ... $\frac{1}{10}$ of all the money that Ceri had was £2?

Page 4

The Language of Maths

- This activity involves children finding halves and quarters of numbers.
- It is recommended that you play the game with the children before they play it by themselves.
- If appropriate, before playing the game, go through each of the 12 statements with the children. Help the children to work out the answer to each of the statements and write it on the board.
- As the children take turns to play the game, encourage them to say the related fraction calculation, e.g. *Half of 8 is 4.*

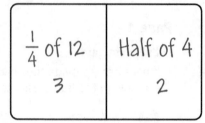

AfL

- Tell me two numbers where one of the numbers is half the other number.
- Tell me two numbers where one of the numbers is one quarter of the other number.
- How many cherries did Jack eat? How many did he have to start with? How did you work that out?
- What is a half of 16?
- What is one quarter of 16? If one quarter of 16 is 4, what do you think three quarters of 16 is?
- Who ate more pizza? How do you know?
- How did you work out how much money Jake / Ceri has altogether?

Answers

Page 1

Let's Investigate
Results of the investigation will vary.

Money Matters
5p is half of 10p.
10p is half of 20p.
50p is half of £1.
£1 is half of £2.

5p is one quarter of 20p.
50p is one quarter of £2.

Page 2

The Puzzler
Jack ate 7 cherries.
Jack started with 14 cherries.

Jill ate 6 cherries.
Jill started with 12 cherries.

What's the Problem?
There are 16 bees.
If $\frac{1}{2}$ fly away there would be 8 bees left.
If $\frac{1}{4}$ fly away there would be 12 bees left.

Page 3

The Puzzler

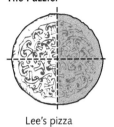 

Lee ate more pizza.

Lee's pizza   Amy's pizza

Money Matters
Jake has £6.
Ceri has £8.

Page 4

The Language of Maths
No answer required.

Inquisitive ant

third
If something is divided into three equal pieces or groups, each part is called a third.

Length and height

Prerequisites for learning

- Describe, estimate, measure and compare objects, choosing and using suitable uniform non-standard or standard units and measuring instruments
- Use a ruler to draw and measure lines

Resources

pencil and paper

Resource sheet 2: My notes (optional)

Resource sheet 3: Pupil self assessment booklet (optional)

interlocking cubes

ruler

string or wool

scissors

Teaching support

Page 1

Let's Investigate

- If appropriate, this activity can be used to informally introduce children to the concept of perimeter.
- It is recommended that children work in pairs on this activity as it involves having to carefully hold the string in place around the 'perimeter' of each of the shapes.
- Ask the children to draw some shapes of their own and compare the shapes' 'perimeters'.

Page 2

Around the World

- Before the children actually count the number of footsteps each of the bears has taken, encourage them to first make an estimate of which bear they think takes the most and least footsteps to get to the honeypot.
- When the children have finished the activity, ask them to answer each of the following questions:
  - How many more steps did baby bear take than mother bear?
  - How many fewer steps did father bear take than baby bear?
  - Who took more steps: father bear or mother bear? How many more?

Page 3

At Home

- It is recommended that children have completed the Around the World activity on page 2 before starting this activity.
- The outcomes of this activity will vary depending on individual children's proximity to their nearest shop. Some children may be able to count the actual number of steps it takes to walk from their front door to the nearest shop. Other children will only be expected to, with the help of an adult, make an estimation.
- Once the children have completed this activity, provide an opportunity for children to discuss their results and whether or not their answer is the actual number of steps or an estimation, and why this is.

Focus on Science

- It is recommended that children work in pairs or as a group on this investigation.
- Prior to setting the children off to work independently, you may wish to discuss with them how they might go about finding out if their (and other children's) handspan or the distance around their wrist is the longer.
- Ensure the children make and write down a prediction before they carry out the investigation.
- Once the children have completed the activity, discuss with them their investigation methods and their results.

Page 4

The Puzzler

- If the children have previously answered the first The Puzzler activity on page 3 of Issue 20 – Fractions, you may like to discuss with them the similarities between the two activities.

- Provide the children with interlocking cubes to make the towers.

At Home

- Once the children have completed the investigation, ensure that there is an opportunity in class for pairs or groups of children to discuss their results.

- If more appropriate, the children can complete this activity in class.

AfL

- How do you use a ruler to measure something?

- How did you measure the sides of these shapes? What were you measuring when you did this?

- Could you tell which bear took the most / least footsteps just by looking? Did you count to check? Were you right?

- How many steps is it from your front door to the nearest shop? Did you walk from your front door to the shop or did you do something else? What did you do?

- Were the number of steps that you took / estimated more or less than an adult? Why do you think this is?

- Which was longer – your handspan or the distance around your wrist? Was this the same for everyone?

- How did you know how many cubes were in Charlotte's tower?

Answers

Page 1

Let's Investigate
The ☐ is 9 cm.
The ○ is 10 cm.
The △ is 12 cm.
The ▭ is 12 cm.

Page 2

Around the World
The baby bear takes the most steps to the honeypot – 35 steps.
The father bear takes the least steps to the honeypot – 15 steps.

Page 3

At Home
Results of the investigation will vary.

Focus on Science
Results of the investigation will vary.

Page 4

The Puzzler
Charlotte would need 10 cubes to make a tower twice the height of her tower.
Charlotte would need 15 cubes to make a tower three times the height of her tower.
Charlotte used 3 cubes to build her second tower.

At Home
Results of the investigation will vary.

Inquisitive ant

distance
The length of space between two people, places or things.

Issue 23

Weight and mass

Prerequisites for learning

- Describe, estimate, weigh and compare objects, choosing and using suitable uniform non-standard or standard units and measuring instruments
- Read the numbered divisions on a scale, and interpret the divisions between them
- Solve logic puzzles

Resources

pencil and paper

Resource sheet 2: My notes (optional)

Resource sheet 3: Pupil self assessment booklet (optional)

scale balance

measuring scales

book

1 kg weight

0–9 dice

spoon

more than 1 kg of rice

more than 1 kg of pasta or sugar or flour

Teaching support

Page 1

Looking for Patterns

- These logic problems can be solved in various ways. However, all methods are based on identifying patterns and relationships. Ensure the children can interpret the two balances at the top of the activity, and that they understand how two stars weigh the same as one cross, and three stars weigh the same as one heart. Once children fully understand this, they should then be able to work out how many stars balance each of the first four scales. They should then be able to apply this knowledge to balance the final two scales.

- This activity is similar to the Looking for Patterns activity on page 3. However, it is slightly easier in that there is no numerical value assigned to the shapes. It is therefore recommended that children complete this activity before starting on the page 3 Looking for Patterns activity.

Let's Investigate

- Once the children have completed this activity, ensure there is an opportunity for pairs or groups to discuss their choices.

- What is the lightest object in school / at home? What is the heaviest object in school / at home?

Page 2

Focus on Science

- This activity is designed to reinforce children's understanding of the vocabulary of two of the standard units for weight – kilogram and gram.

- This activity is simply about calculating in the context of weight.

- With reference to the last two shapes, ensure the children realise that the total weight of each shape is not simply the number of blocks that can be seen. It also includes those that cannot be seen.

Let's Investigate

- There are three aspects to this activity. Firstly, estimating how heavy a set of objects are and placing them in order heaviest to lightest. Secondly, using the scale balance to place objects in order by weight, and finally explaining why some objects were harder to order than others, e.g. because they were similar to each other in weight / because their size belied their weight / because you had to use one / two hands.

Page 3

Looking for Patterns

- This activity is similar to the 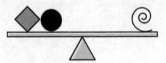 Looking for Patterns activity on page 1. However, it is slightly more difficult in that each of the shapes have been assigned a numerical value. It is therefore recommended that children complete the 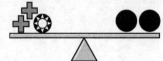 Looking for Patterns activity on page 1 before starting on this activity.

- Given that the children know the value of eight different shapes, ask them to use this information to draw some sets of scales that balance, e.g.

Let's Investigate

- Ensure children choose a suitable book (and a second object) for this investigation. That is, one that is not too light, so that it registers very little on the measuring scales; yet one that is not too heavy, where 10 of them makes the activity unmanageable. It is also recommended that, if possible, when choosing a book, children choose one that is similar in weight to nine other books.

- Once the children have weighed one book (and one of the second objects), ensure that they first make an estimation of what they think the weight of ten of the books (and other object) is before they weigh them.

Page 4

Let's Investigate

- There are two aspects to this activity. Firstly, playing the game, and secondly, discussing and reasoning, if and how, the game might be quicker or longer if a different substance is used.

- Before setting the children off to play the game independently, ensure that they are familiar with the rules of the game.

At Home

- Once the children have completed the investigation, ensure that there is an opportunity in class for pairs or groups of children to discuss their results.

- If more appropriate, the children can complete this activity in class.

AfL

- How did you work out how many stars needed to go on this set of scales? What patterns did you notice as you were doing this?
- Tell me something lighter / heavier than this chair.
- How did you work out the answer to this puzzle? What patterns did you notice that helped you?
- How did the game change when you played it with pasta / sugar / flour rather than with rice? Is this what you expected?

Answers

Page 1

Looking for Patterns

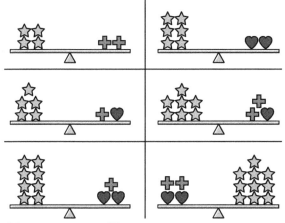

Other answers are possible.

Let's Investigate
Results of the investigation will vary.

Page 2

Focus on Science

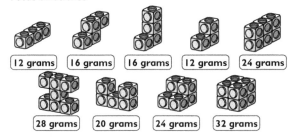

Let's Investigate
Results of the investigation will vary.

Page 3

Looking for Patterns

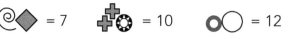

Let's Investigate
Results of the investigation will vary.

Page 4

Let's Investigate
Explanations will vary. However, there should be some mention of the fact that the heavier the foodstuff used, the quicker the game.

At Home
Results of the investigation will vary.

Inquisitive ant balance

1. The even distribution of weight.
2. An instrument for weighing.

Issue 24

Capacity and volume

Prerequisites for learning

- Describe, estimate, measure and compare objects, choosing and using suitable uniform non-standard or standard units and measuring instruments
- Read the numbered divisions on a scale, and interpret the divisions between them

Resources

pencil and paper

Resource sheet 2: My notes (optional)

Resource sheet 3: Pupil self assessment booklet (optional)

matchbox (optional)

access to a tap

bowl

1 litre measuring jug

collection of small objects such as cubes, marbles, paper clips, pasta shells

large bottle of mineral water or fizzy drink

paper cups

collection of small containers such as yoghurt pot, paper cup, egg cup, paint pot

material for making a poster, such as large sheet of paper, colouring materials, magazines (optional)

Teaching support

Page 1

Let's Investigate

- This activity is designed to teach children that capacity is about the amount that something contains, and that it is not always just about the amount of water or liquid in a jug or container.

- It is recommended that you have available a matchbox for the children to refer to as they undertake this activity.

- Once the children have completed this activity, arrange them into pairs or groups and ask them to compare and discuss their lists.

Let's Investigate

- Before setting the children off to carry out this investigation independently, it is recommended that you spend some time discussing the activity with them, highlighting the following:

  - how to work as a pair to collect the water in their cupped hands
  - how to carefully tip the water from their hands into the bowl
  - how to carefully pour the water from the bowl into the measuring jug.

- Once the children have completed the activity, ask them to write about their results.

Page 2

Let's Investigate

- This activity is designed to teach children that capacity is about the amount that something contains, and that it is not always just about the amount of water or liquid in a jug or container.

- Before setting the children off to carry out this investigation independently, it is recommended that you spend some time discussing the activity with them, highlighting the following:

  - a suitable small object to use
  - how to organise the collection of the data
  - how to record the data in the table.

Let's Investigate

- Ensure the children make a prediction before using the bottle and cups to carry out the investigation.
- To save on resources, it is recommended that children work in pairs or groups on this activity.
- When the children have completed this activity, provide them with eight paper cups. Ask them to work out how many bottles of mineral water or fizzy drink they would need to completely fill all eight cups.

Page 3

Focus on Science

- This activity is designed to consolidate children's ability to estimate capacity.
- You may wish to arrange the children into pairs or groups to undertake this activity.
- Encourage the children to draw or write about their results.
- Once the children have completed the activity, discuss the results with them. Did their estimates become more accurate as they progressed through the activity?

At Home

- Once the children have completed the investigation, ensure that there is an opportunity in class for pairs or groups of children to discuss their results.
- If more appropriate, the children can complete this activity in class.

Page 4

Focus on Science

- This activity is designed to teach children that capacity is about the amount that something contains, and that it is not always just about the amount of water or liquid in a jug or container. It also consolidates children's ability to estimate capacity.
- Once the children have completed the activity, discuss the results with them. Did their estimates become more accurate as they progressed through the activity?

The Language of Maths

- You may wish to ask the children to do this activity at home along with the ⌂ At Home activity on page 3.

- You may wish to ask the children to make a poster displaying what they have found out about litres and pints. They could also incorporate the Inquisitive ant activity mentioning gallons. Perhaps they could use drawings, pictures or photos to illustrate their poster.

AfL

- Tell me some of the things on your list.
- How did you measure how much water you could hold in your hands?
- Whose handful has the greatest capacity? How sure are you of your results?
- What was tricky about this experiment? What did you have to do to make sure that you did it properly?
- How close was your guess / estimate?
- Did you get better as you measured more things? Why do you think this is?
- What does the word 'litre' refer to? What about the word 'pint'? How are these two words the same? How are they different?

Answers

Page 1

Let's Investigate
Lists will vary.

Let's Investigate
Results of the investigation will vary.

Page 2

Let's Investigate
Results of the investigation will vary.

Let's Investigate
Results of the investigation will vary.

Page 3

Focus on Science
Results of the investigation will vary.

At Home
Lists will vary.

Page 4

Focus on Science
Results of the investigation will vary.

The Language of Maths
Litres and pints are both units of measure for capacity.
Litres are a metric measure whereas pints are an
imperial measure.
1 litre is equal to about $1\frac{3}{4}$ pints or 1 pint is equal to a little more than $\frac{1}{2}$ litre.

Inquisitive ant

gallon
Standard unit of measure for capacity. It is equivalent to 8 pints or approximately 4·5 litres.

Prerequisites for learning

- Use vocabulary related to time
- Know the days of the week and months of the year
- Read and show the time to the hour and half hour
- Identify time intervals

Resources

pencil and paper
Resource sheet 2: My notes (optional)
Resource sheet 3: Pupil self assessment booklet (optional)
Resource sheet 10: Times of the day
stopwatch or clock with a seconds hand
interlocking cubes

Teaching support

Page 1

The Language of Maths

- This activity is designed to be open-ended and allow children to choose times of the day, or more likely events during the day, that are memorable to them.
- Encourage the children to write times that they are confident with. Most children should be able to read and write the time to the hour and half hour on an analogue clock. If children are also able to read and write the time to the quarter hour, or even five or one minute intervals, then encourage them to use these times. However, it is more likely that for most children, their memorable events will occur close to the hour or half hour.
- Children need to have completed this activity before starting on the following 🏠 At Home activity.

At Home

- Children will need to have completed the previous 🐜 The Language of Maths activity before starting on this activity.
- Once the children have completed the investigation, ensure that there is an opportunity in class for pairs or groups of children to discuss their results.

Page 2

What's the Problem?

- Suggest the children draw a number line (time-line) to help them work out the answers to the questions, e.g.

- In what year was Lucy born?

The Language of Maths

- Provide the children with one of the strips of five clocks from Resource sheet 10: Times of the day.

Ask them to show each of the new times on the analogue clocks. If appropriate, also ask them to write each of these times in digital notation in the box underneath the corresponding analogue clock.

- What if the clock shows quarter to 5?

Page 3

The Language of Maths

- Ensure the children understand the abbreviations for the seven days of the week.
- Do not spend too much time explaining the calendar to the children. This activity is designed to provide an opportunity for the children to discover for themselves how a calendar works.
- When the children have finished, discuss with them the patterns they notice on the calendar. Is this the same for all months of the year? How are the months the same? How are they different?

Let's Investigate

- Remind the children that there are two parts to this activity. Firstly, making a list of things that take about one minute or less to do, and secondly finding out how many of each of the activities listed they can do in one minute.

- For the second part of this activity suggest the children work in pairs, taking turns to be the timekeeper and the one doing each of the activities.

Page 4

What's the Problem?

- If necessary, draw children's attention to the days of the week labelling at the top of the calendar in
   The Language of Maths activity on page 3. Alternatively, draw for the children a simple diagram similar to the one below so that they can better see the cyclical nature of the days of the week.

The Language of Maths

- When the children have written as much as they can on their yearly cycle, arrange them into pairs or groups to compare and discuss their diagrams. Individual children can add events to their respective diagram if they also have some meaning for them.

AfL

- Read me the times you drew on these clocks.
- How did you work out the answer to this problem?
- How much time has passed from 8 o'clock in the morning until 11 o'clock in the morning? What about between 8 o'clock in the morning until 3 o'clock in the afternoon?
- What time is it now? What time was it an hour ago? What time will it be in one hours' time? What about in three hours' time?
- Look at this calendar. What day of the week is it on September 17th? How many Mondays are there in September? What date is the first Sunday in September?
- Tell me some of the things that take about one minute to do.
- Which months were easy to think of things to write / draw about? Which were not so easy?

Answers

Page 1

The Language of Maths
Clocks and descriptions will vary.

At Home
Clocks and descriptions will vary.

Page 2

What's the Problem?
Lucy was 3 years old in 2010.
She will be 17 years old in 2024.

The Language of Maths
2 hours after: $\frac{1}{2}$ past 6

5 hours after: $\frac{1}{2}$ past 9
$3\frac{1}{2}$ hours after: 8 o'clock
6 hours before: $\frac{1}{2}$ past 10
$4\frac{1}{2}$ hours before: 12 o'clock

Page 3

The Language of Maths
Questions will vary.

Let's Investigate
Results of the investigation will vary.

Page 4

What's the Problem?
4 days from now: Thursday   4 days ago: Wednesday
9 days from now: Tuesday   9 days ago: Friday
12 days from now: Friday   12 days ago: Tuesday
16 days from now: Tuesday   16 days ago: Friday

The Language of Maths
Completed diagrams will vary.

Inquisitive ant

annual
Occurring once every year.

Measurement

Prerequisites for learning

- Describe, estimate, measure, weigh and compare objects, choosing and using suitable uniform non-standard or standard units and measuring instruments
- Read the numbered divisions on a scale, and interpret the divisions between them
- Use vocabulary related to time
- Identify time intervals
- Solve logic puzzles

Resources

pencil and paper

Resource sheet 2: My notes (optional)

Resource sheet 3: Pupil self assessment booklet (optional)

Resource sheet 6: Dogs, cats and chickens

collection of different sized containers

measuring jug

access to water

scissors

glue

ice cube tray

salt

sugar

fruit juice

fizzy drink

Teaching support

Page 1

At Home

- Once the children have completed the investigation, ensure that there is an opportunity in class for pairs or groups of children to discuss their results. Who, amongst the children, travels furthest to and from school? Who travels the shortest distance? Who has a family member who travels the longest / shortest distance to school / work? Which family travels the most during a week? Why is this?

Page 2

Let's Investigate

- It is recommended that children work in pairs on this activity.
- There are two aspects to this activity. The first involves the children identifying two different containers where one is approximately half the capacity of the other. This requires the children to make approximations. Children are not expected to have found two containers where one is *exactly* half the capacity of the other – approximately half is acceptable.
- The second aspect of this activity involves the children devising a way of checking the accuracy of their approximations. This will require the children to choose and use appropriate non-standard (or standard) measuring equipment and units, and using these accurately.

Looking for Patterns

- It is recommended that children work in pairs on this activity.
- These logic problems can be solved in various ways. However, all methods are based on identifying patterns and relationships. Ensure the children can interpret the two balances in the Issue, and that they understand how three cats weigh the same as one dog, and two chickens weigh the same as one cat. Once children fully understand this, they should then be able to balance the four scales on the Resource sheet.

- If children are having difficulty, draw an empty scale balance on a piece of paper. Referring to Resource sheet 6: Dogs, cats and chickens, put a dog on one side of the blank scale and ask children how many cats are needed on the other side to balance the scale (3). Now clear the scale and put a cat on one side and ask how many chickens are needed to balance the scale (2). Clear the scale and put three cats on one side of it. Pointing to the balance in the Issue showing 1 cat = 2 chickens, ask: *How many chickens are needed to balance these?* (6). Now take a dog and, pointing to the balance in the Issue showing 1 dog = 3 cats, say: *We know that 1 dog balances 3 cats, so we can replace these 3 cats with 1 dog.* Replace the cats with the dog. Ask: *How many chickens balance 1 dog?*

Page 3

At Home

- It is recommended that children complete the Inquisitive ant activity before starting on this activity.

- Once the children have completed the activity, ensure that there is an opportunity in class for pairs or groups of children to share and discuss their time-lines.

Let's Investigate

- Once the children have completed the investigation, arrange them into pairs or groups and ask them to compare and discuss their tables. Then ask the children to think about how they could sort all the objects on their lists. Could they sort them in more than one way? If appropriate, ask the children to write about their combined, sorted lists.

Page 4

Focus on Science

- Prior to setting the children off to work independently on this activity, ensure they understand what they are required to do.
- Encourage the children to think carefully about how they are going to monitor and measure the dissolving ice cubes and also how to display their results.
- Children will probably need to undertake this activity over two days. The first day making their ice cubes and allowing them to freeze overnight. The second day finding out which ice cubes melt the quickest / slowest.
- Once the children have completed the activity, ask them to think about how their results might be different if they did this experiment at a different time of the day or year.

AfL

- Why do you think that this container holds half the capacity of this container?
- What did you do to check?
- Explain to me why these scales balance.
- Tell me about your time-line.
- Did you find more things to measure the length of something, the weight of something or how much something holds? Why do you think this is?
- Which ice cube melted the quickest / slowest? What did you do to find this out?
- Explain your results to me.

Answers

Page 1

At Home
Results of the investigation will vary.

Page 2

Let's Investigate
Results of the investigation will vary.

Looking for Patterns
2 cats   6 chickens   1 dog   7 cats

Page 3

At Home
Time-lines will vary.

Let's Investigate
Results of the investigation will vary.

Page 4

Focus on Science
Results of the investigation will vary.

Inquisitive ant

time-line
A way of displaying a list of events in the order that they happen (chronological order).

Measurement

Prerequisites for learning

- Describe, estimate, measure, weigh and compare objects, choosing and using suitable uniform non-standard or standard units and measuring instruments
- Read the numbered divisions on a scale, and interpret the divisions between them
- Use vocabulary related to time
- Identify time intervals

Resources

pencil and paper
Resource sheet 2: My notes (optional)
Resource sheet 3: Pupil self assessment booklet (optional)
wooden beads
laces or string
measuring scales
interlocking cubes
paintbrush
collection of different sponges
access to water
large bowl
measuring jug

Teaching support

Page 1

Construct

- There are two aspects to this activity. Firstly, making a necklace from wooden beads, weighing as near to 200 grams as is possible. Secondly, the children use their knowledge of how many beads were needed to make the wooden necklace, deciding whether they would need to use more or fewer interlocking cubes to make a cube necklace also weighing 200 grams.
- Children need to be familiar with the standard unit of weight – grams. Therefore, it is recommended that children complete the Inquisitive ant activity before starting on this activity.
- Children also need to realise that it may not be possible to make necklaces weighing exactly 200 grams. They are aiming to make them as near to 200 grams as is possible.

Page 2

The Language of Maths

- This, and the following activity, are designed to consolidate children's understanding of the comparative language of measures.
- Can the children find more than one object for each of the three comparative statements?
- Ask the children to write statements comparing the length, weight or capacity of two, or more, objects or containers.
- When the children have completed the activity, arrange them into pairs or groups to compare and discuss their results.

The Language of Maths

- This, and the previous activity, are designed to consolidate children's understanding of the comparative language of measures.
- When the children have completed the activity, arrange them into pairs or groups to compare and discuss their results.

Page 3

Focus on Science

- Prior to setting the children off to work independently on this activity, ensure they understand what they are required to do.
- Encourage the children to think carefully about how they are going to measure the amount of water that each sponge holds and also how to display their results. Children also need to ensure that the amount of soaking / absorption time for each sponge is the same.
- When the children have completed the activity, discuss with them their results and reasoning.

Money Matters

- You may wish to arrange the children into pairs or groups for this activity so that they can share their thoughts and discuss their reasoning.

Page 4

At Home

- Prior to asking the children to complete this activity at home, you may wish to use the Chinese Calendar to show what Chinese year the children and yourself were born.
- As the Chinese New Year falls on a different day each year, a date between January 21 and February 20, if a person's birthday is before that date, they count as the previous year's animal. Therefore there may be some discrepancy in some of the children's results. However, the important aspect of this activity is that children are able to see and use the cyclical nature of the Chinese Calendar.
- When the children have completed the activity, ensure that there is an opportunity in class for pairs or groups of children to discuss their results.

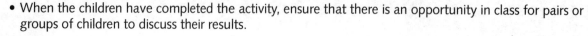

AfL

- How close to 200 grams is your necklace? Show me.
- Can you think of something else that is longer than a pencil, but shorter than a ruler?
- Look at this paintbrush. How does the length of this paintbrush compare with some other objects in the classroom?
- Can you tell me some things that are a little / a lot lighter than this table? What about some things that are a little / a lot heavier than this table? Tell me something that you think might weigh about the same as this table.
- What did you find out about the different sponges? Was there a big difference in how much water they can each hold? Which sponge held the most / least water? Did you think that one would hold the most / least? Did the largest sponge hold the most water? Did the smallest sponge hold the least water? Why do you think that some sponges held more water than others?
- Is money a measure? Why / Why not?
- According to the Chinese Calendar what year was it in 2010?
- When will it be the next Year of the Dragon?

Answers

Page 1

Construct
Results of the investigation will vary. However, children's explanations should focus on the fact that the lighter the object used to make the necklace, the more of them are needed to make a necklace of 200 grams.

Page 2

The Language of Maths
Results of the investigation will vary.

The Language of Maths
Results of the investigation will vary.

Page 3

Focus on Science
Results of the investigation will vary.

Money Matters
Money is a measure.
Children's reasoning will vary.

Page 4

At Home
Results of the investigation will vary.

Inquisitive ant

gram
A metric unit of measure for mass (or weight).

Issue 28

2-D shapes

Prerequisites for learning

- Identify patterns and relationships involving shapes
- Recognise and name common 2-D shapes and describe their features
- Use 2-D shapes to make patterns and pictures
- Identify shapes from pictures of them in different positions and orientations
- Use concrete objects and pictorial representations to support the addition of a one-digit number or a multiple of 10 to a one-digit or two-digit number

Resources

pencil and paper

Resource sheet 2: My notes (optional)

Resource sheet 3: Pupil self assessment booklet (optional)

Resource sheet 11: Greek cross puzzles

Resource sheet 12: 2-D shapes

Resource sheet 13: Triangle shapes

Resource sheet 19: 2 cm squared paper

scissors

ruler

calculator (optional)

Teaching support

Page 1

In the Past

- If necessary, cut out each Greek cross from Resource sheet 11. However, leave the children to cut the two lines that cut across each Greek cross.

The Puzzler

- If necessary, discuss with the children the six different variables in these puzzles, i.e. square, circle, triangle, grey shading, grid lines and dots.

- Discuss with the children how they need to look for the similarities and differences in each column and row.

- Tell the children that the six shapes climbing over the two grids are the missing shapes. Can they work out which shape belongs where?

- Children design a similar puzzle for a friend to solve.

Page 2

Looking for Patterns

- If children cannot find all eight triangles, arrange them into pairs to compare the triangles that they have each found so far.

Let's Investigate

- Ensure children realise that one side of a shape must completely touch another side of another shape, e.g.

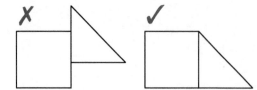

- Ask the children to name each of the shapes they have made.

- Provide the children with two copies of Resource sheet 12: 2-D shapes, and ask them to investigate what different shapes they can make.

- Encourage children to use 2 cm squared paper (Resource sheet 19) and a ruler to draw their shapes.

176

Page 3

Let's Investigate

- It is recommended that children work in pairs on this activity.
- For each set of three puzzles, the first puzzle in each set should help children identify the solutions to the remaining two puzzles in each set (see Answers). You may wish to inform children of this fact.

The Puzzler

- Make sure that the children understand that before they work out the total value of each of the compound shapes they should first divide each shape into its smaller shapes, e.g.

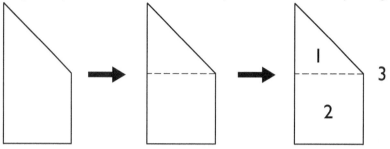

- If necessary, allow the children to use a calculator to work out the total value of each shape.

Page 4

Let's Investigate

- Children require only one of the triangular grids from Resource sheet 13: Triangle shapes, for this activity. The other grid is used for the following 🐜 Construct activity.
- The triangular grids are actually isometric grids. This activity introduces children to using this type of mathematical paper in a fun and interesting way.
- Ensure the children realise that the following two shapes are considered the same – they are just a transformation of each other.

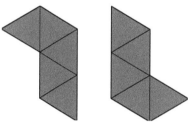

- Children need to have completed this activity before starting on the following 🐜 Construct activity.

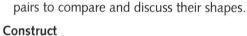
- Once the children have completed this activity, arrange them into pairs to compare and discuss their shapes.

Construct

- Children require only one of the triangular grids from Resource sheet 13: Triangle shapes, for this activity. The other grid is used for the previous 🦋 Let's Investigate activity.
- Children need to have completed the previous 🦋 Let's Investigate activity before starting on this activity.

- You may wish the children to work in pairs on this activity.

AfL

- Which of these two puzzles was easier? Why?
- Why does this shape belong here? Why not this shape?
- Which triangles were tricky to find?
- What shape have you made?
- How did knowing the answer to this puzzle, help you work out the answer to the next one?
- What is the value of this shape? How did you work it out?
- Are these shapes the same or different? How are they the same? How are they different?
- Were you able to colour the whole grid? Show me how. Do you think you could have coloured it differently and still be right? How?

Answers

Page 1

In the Past

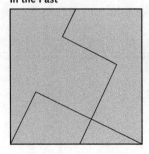 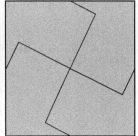

The Puzzler

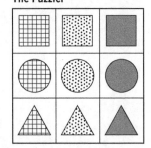 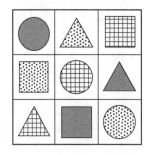

Page 2

Looking for Patterns

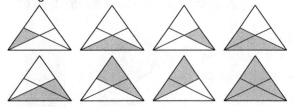

Let's Investigate
Drawings of shapes will vary.

Page 3

Let's Investigate

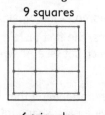 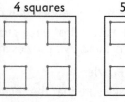 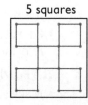

9 squares   4 squares   5 squares

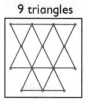 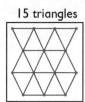

6 triangles   9 triangles   15 triangles

Other solutions are possible.

The Puzzler

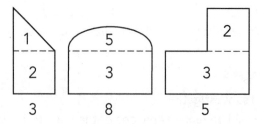

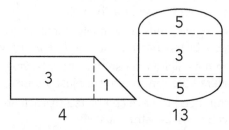

Page 4

Let's Investigate
Shapes will vary.

Construct
Given that there are 40 triangles, and each of the shapes is made from 5 triangles, it is possible to colour the entire grid.

Inquisitive ant

value
1. The numerical quantity given to a mathematical symbol.
2. The material or monetary worth of something.

Issue 29

3-D shapes

Prerequisites for learning

- Identify patterns and relationships involving shapes
- Recognise and name common 3-D shapes and describe their features
- Use 3-D shapes to make patterns, pictures and models
- Identify shapes in different positions and orientations
- Sort, make and describe shapes, referring to their properties
- Identify reflective symmetry
- Recognise and use everyday language to describe the position of objects

Resources

pencil and paper

Resource sheet 2: My notes (optional)

Resource sheet 3: Pupil self assessment booklet (optional)

Resource sheet 14: House

box

scissors

interlocking cubes

glue

ruler

coloured pencils

3-D geometric shapes, including a large number of rectangular and triangular prisms

large sheet of paper

drawing materials

Teaching support

Page 1

Construct

- This activity requires the children to cut out, assemble and decorate their house. Some children may need assistance with the manual dexterity that is required for this activity. If necessary, ask the children to work in pairs to complete their house, providing assistance to each other when and where necessary.
- Children need to have completed this activity before starting the 🐜 Construct activity on page 3.

Let's Investigate

- Before starting this activity, ensure that you make the children aware of the health and safety implications of cutting their box.
- An empty tissue box is an ideal size box for this activity.
- You may wish to suggest to the children that they think carefully about how they are going to cut their box in half so that both halves are the same – symmetrical – before they actually cut it.
- You may also wish to work together with the children on this activity, asking them to draw lines to indicate where they think the box should be cut, with you actually doing the cutting for them.
- Once pairs have cut their box, arrange them into groups to compare and discuss their box with others.

Page 2

Let's Investigate

- Ensure children realise that the following four shapes are considered the same – they are just different transformations of each other.

At Home

- Once the children have played the game at home, ensure that there is an opportunity in class for pairs or groups of children to discuss the game and also what questions were good questions to ask.

Page 3

Construct

- Children need to have completed the Construct activity on page 1 before starting this activity.

- There are three different aspects to this activity. Firstly, using the blocks to make a simple house shape similar to the one the children constructed in the Construct activity on page 1. Secondly, drawing and labelling their 'block' house. Finally, constructing, drawing and labelling a larger house than the previous one.

- Ensure children have a range of different sized cuboids and triangular prisms. Most children will be able to construct a simple house shape, but may need help making a larger one.

The Language of Maths

- This activity requires the children to visualise each of the 3-D shapes named.

- If necessary, read through the names of the shapes with the children and show them the matching 3-D geometric shape.

Page 4

Looking for Patterns

- Once the children have completed this activity go through each shape and ask them to tell you how the shape has been moved, e.g.

From  to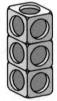

> This shape moved anti-clockwise a quarter of a turn.

AfL

- Show me your house. What shapes can you see in your house? What 3-D shapes is it made from?
- How else could you have cut your box?
- What does the word 'symmetrical' mean?
- What were good questions to ask to try and 'Hunt the 3-D shape'?
- Are these shapes the same or different? How are they the same? How are they different?
- What can you tell me about the shapes of the faces in a cuboid?
- Point to a shape that is the same as this shape. How has this shape been moved?
- Are these two shapes the same or different? How can you tell?

Answers

Page 1

Construct
The completed house should look as follows:

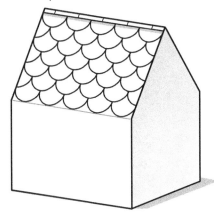

Let's Investigate
Results of the investigation will vary.

Page 2

Let's Investigate

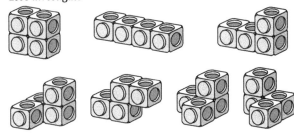

At Home
Results of the investigation will vary.

Page 3

Construct
Shapes will vary.

The Language of Maths

Note: Cuboids can have square and rectangular faces or rectangular faces only. Therefore, accept the answer above without the line drawn from the word 'cuboid' to the illustration of the square.

Page 4

Looking for Patterns

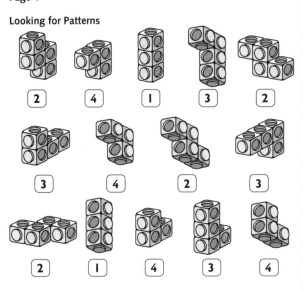

Inquisitive ant

3-D
Abbreviation of *three-dimensional*. A solid shape with dimensions of height, width and depth.

Patterns

Prerequisites for learning

- Recognise and create repeating patterns with objects and with shapes
- Identify symmetry in patterns and 2-D shapes

Resources

pencil and paper

Resource sheet 2: My notes (optional)

Resource sheet 3: Pupil self assessment booklet (optional)

Resource sheet 15: Symmetrical patterns

Resource sheet 16: Symmetrical game

Resource sheet 19: 2 cm squared paper (optional)

ruler

coloured pencils

counters all the same colour

counters in a second colour (optional)

Teaching support

Page 1

Let's Investigate

- Ensure children understand the concept of symmetry before undertaking this activity. Given this, you may wish the children to complete the Inquisitive ant (symmetrical) activity before starting on this activity.
- Still colouring only eight squares, suggest the children use two different colours in their symmetrical pattern.
- Provide the children with 2 cm squared paper (Resource sheet 19) and ask them to draw designs with diagonal symmetry.

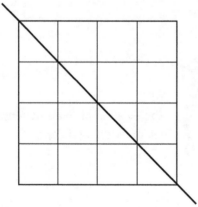

Page 2

Construct

- When the children have completed their rug pattern, arrange them into pairs or groups. Ask the children to swap designs and take turns to describe the pattern in each other's rug.

Page 3

Looking for Patterns

- Allow the children to use red and blue interlocking cubes to make the towers before they colour them on the Issue. Altogether children will need 12 red and 12 blue interlocking cubes to make all eight towers.

Looking for Patterns

- Before setting the children off to play the game by themselves, ensure they fully understand how to play the game. Also remind the children that they need to take turns at being the player who puts the counters on the grey dots.

- Provide the children with 32 counters in two different colours, i.e. 16 of one colour and 16 of another colour.

Page 4

Construct

- This activity involves the children drawing the reflection of nine different shapes. There are purposely no grid lines for this activity. The children are required to carefully draw each shape's reflection taking into account both the positioning and orientation of the reflected half of the shape as well as its size.

AfL

- What does the word 'symmetry' mean?
- How are these shapes symmetrical?
- Describe your rug / paper pattern to me.
- What makes this pattern symmetrical?
- What patterns did you notice as you were colouring the blocks?

Answers

Page 1

Let's Investigate
Symmetrical designs will vary.

Page 2

Construct
Rug designs will vary.

Page 3

Looking for Patterns

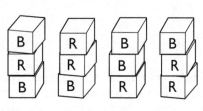

Looking for Patterns
No answer required.

Construct

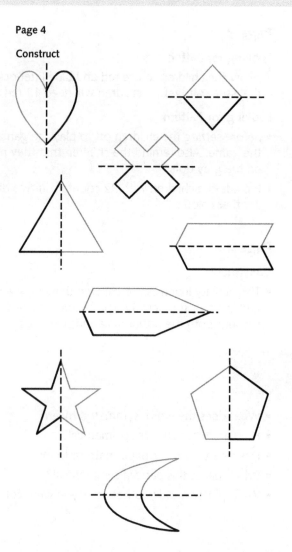

Inquisitive ant

symmetrical
When both halves of a shape match each other as if seen in a mirror, then the shape is said to be symmetrical.

Issue 31

Position and direction

Prerequisites for learning

- Describe simple patterns and relationships involving shapes
- Visualise and use everyday language to describe the position of objects and direction
- Follow and give instructions involving position, direction and movement
- Solve logic puzzles
- Use ordinal numbers in different contexts

Resources

pencil and paper

Resource sheet 2: My notes (optional)

Resource sheet 3: Pupil self assessment booklet (optional)

Resource sheet 7: Bookshelf (two copies per child)

scissors

glue

A4 paper

coloured pencils

Teaching support

Page 1

At Home

- Once the children have completed the investigation, ensure that there is an opportunity in class for pairs or groups of children to discuss their results.
- If more appropriate, the children can complete this activity in class.

The Puzzler

- What if Ros were to join the group and sit opposite Lee? How would the clues need to be changed?

Page 2

The Language of Maths

- Prior to the activity, ensure the children are familiar with the terms 'above', 'below', 'to the left' and 'to the right'.
- It is recommended that you go through the placing of the drum with the children, i.e. the first instruction, before setting them off to work independently on the activity.
- Once you have checked that the toys are in the correct place, allow the children to glue the toys in place and cut out the bookshelf.
- When the children have completed their bookshelf arrange them into pairs. Ask the children to take turns to ask each other questions about their bookshelves. For example, *what is below the doll? Point to the toy that is between the car and the plane. What is between the toy soldier and the train?*

The Language of Maths

- Ensure that children understand that one child secretly places all of their toys in their cupboard and then describes the position of all 12 toys to their partner. Only when this has been done do the children swap roles.
- Suggest children choose only six toys to place in their cupboard, and that they place them all in and around one or other of the corners of the bookshelf.

Page 3

Construct

- Ensure children understand what a tessellating pattern is.
- Children can continue each of these patterns as far across the page as is reasonable, as long as they sufficiently demonstrate that they understand how the pattern is formed.
- Once the children have finished this activity, if appropriate, arrange them into pairs and ask them to walk around the school looking for examples of tessellating patterns.

Page 4

Construct

- If the route from the school office to the children's classroom is too simple (or too complex), then ask them to draw a map for a different route around the school.
- Prior to the children working independently on this activity, you may want to discuss with them useful landmarks to include on their map.
- Encourage the children to draw a rough sketch first, followed by a more detailed and accurate drawing.

- You may wish the children to take into account the distances between various landmarks and be aware of the concept of scale. If necessary, discuss this with them.

The Language of Maths

- Once the children have completed the activity, discuss with them the strategies they used to work out how many children there are standing in the line (one less than the sum of the two given positions).

- Describe your pictures to me.
- How did you work out the answer to this puzzle / problem?
- Tell me some words that we use to describe the position of something. What does … mean?
- What is happening in this pattern?
- Describe your route to me.
- Tell me one thing that you could change on your map to improve it.

Answers

Page 1

At Home
Pictures will vary.

The Puzzler

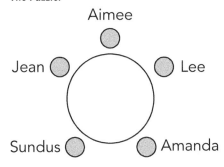

Page 2

The Language of Maths

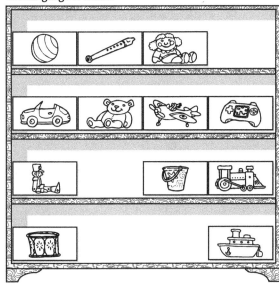

The Language of Maths
Answers will vary.

Page 3

Construct

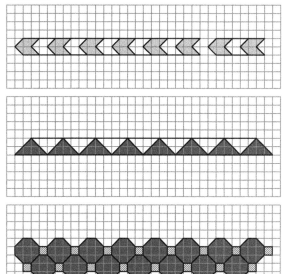

Page 4

Construct
Maps will vary.

The Language of Maths
There are 6 children standing in the line.
There are 9 children standing in the line.
There are 7 children standing in the line.

Inquisitive ant map
A diagram showing the position of things in a given area.

Issue 32

Movement

Prerequisites for learning

- Describe simple patterns and relationships involving shapes
- Identify objects that turn about a point or about a line
- Recognise and make whole, half and quarter turns
- Identify shapes in different positions and orientations
- Understand and use the terms 'clockwise', 'anti-clockwise', 'half turn', 'quarter turn' and 'three-quarter turn'
- Visualise and use everyday language to describe the position of objects and direction
- Follow and give instructions involving position, direction and movement

Resources

pencil and paper
Resource sheet 2: My notes (optional)
Resource sheet 3: Pupil self assessment booklet (optional)
coloured pencils
small Compare Bear (or similar)
coin
1–6 dice
counters

Teaching support

Page 1

The Language of Maths

- Ensure the children are familiar with the terms 'clockwise' and 'anti-clockwise'.
- Before setting the children off to work independently on this activity, you may need to spend some time with them explaining and demonstrating what they are required to do.
- Encourage the children to use the diagram to help them answer the five questions.
- If necessary, provide them with a small Compare Bear (or similar) to represent the child in the middle of the diagram. Explain how they can turn this to help them work out what the child is facing after each turn.

Page 2

Looking for Patterns

- Once the children have completed the activity, discuss with them how the shapes in each pattern have moved, e.g.

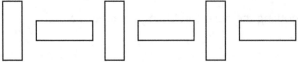

Quarter turn left (or right), Quarter turn left (or right), Quarter turn left (or right), …

 • Ask the children to make some repeating patterns of their own involving the transformations of simple shapes.

The Language of Maths

- Ensure the children are familiar with the terms 'up', 'down', 'to the left' and 'to the right' and how they relate to this activity.
- Children need to complete this activity before starting on the first 🐜 The Language of Maths activity on page 3.

Page 3

The Language of Maths

- Children need to have completed the The Language of Maths activity on page 2 before starting on this activity.

- When the children have completed both this and the The Language of Maths activity on page 2, arrange them into pairs. Provide the children with small counters. Children take turns to put all the counters on the grid (but not diagonally) to form a trail starting at 'Start' to the top of the grid. Their partner then describes how to move along the trail formed by the counters. For example;
  Move up 2 spaces.
  Move to the right 2 spaces.
  Move up 1 space.

The Language of Maths

- Once the children have completed the activity discuss with them how each shape would look after it had moved a quarter turn to the left / clockwise a quarter of a turn.

Page 4

The Puzzler

- Ensure the children are familiar with the terms 'half turn', 'quarter turn right' and 'quarter turn left'.

- Before setting the children off to play the game independently, also ensure that they are familiar with the rules of the game, and in particular how to use the counter diagram with the Compare Bear at the top of the page. You may wish to spend a few minutes playing the game with the children to get them started.

AfL

- Show me what a quarter turn clockwise / anti-clockwise looks like.
- What is another way of saying 'a quarter turn to the right'? What about 'a quarter turn to the left'?
- What is happening to the shapes in this pattern? How are they moving?
- What would these shapes look like after a quarter turn to the right / left?
- When you turn through half a turn does it matter if you turn to the left or to the right / clockwise or anti-clockwise?

Answers

Page 1

The Language of Maths

Facing	After turning
Tables	Windows
Windows	Door
Door	Mat
Mat	Door
Windows	Tables

Page 2

Looking for Patterns

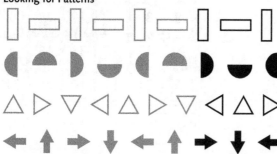

The Language of Maths
23, 33, 3, 7, 17, 15, 6, 12

Page 3

The Language of Maths

Move up 4 spaces [24]

Move to the right 5 spaces [19]

Move down 2 spaces [4]

Move to the left 3 spaces [27]

Move up 2 spaces [35]

Move to the left 1 space [14]

Move down 3 spaces [21]

Move to the right 4 spaces [31]

Looking for Patterns

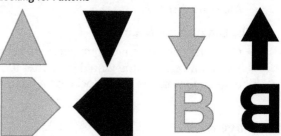

Page 4

The Puzzler
No answer required.

Inquisitive ant

clockwise
Rotating in the same direction as the hands of an analogue clock.

Prerequisites for learning	Resources
• Identify patterns and relationships involving shapes • Recognise and name common 2-D shapes and describe their features • Use 2-D shapes to make patterns and pictures	pencil and paper Resource sheet 2: My notes (optional) Resource sheet 3: Pupil self assessment booklet (optional) Resource sheet 17: Four square shapes (2 copies per child) Resource sheet 19: 2 cm squared paper (2 copies per child) scissors coloured pencils (optional) ruler (optional) selection of 2-D shapes Lego (optional) selection of 3-D shapes (optional) interlocking cubes (optional)

Teaching support

Page 1

Looking for Patterns

• If the children have already completed the Looking for Patterns activity on page 2 of Issue 28: 2-D shapes, then they should find this activity relatively easy.

The Puzzler

• Tell the children that there is more than one solution to this puzzle. Can they find another solution? How are these two solutions the same? How are they different?

Page 2

Looking for Patterns

• This activity introduces children to the idea that sequences are not just about numbers, but can be about almost anything, including shapes.

• Ask the children to design a repeating shape pattern of their own, perhaps using transformations, e.g.

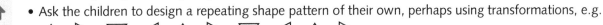

The Language of Maths

• Ensure children can accurately name common 2-D shapes and use a range of appropriate positional language. The correct use of both of these is important in successfully describing and interpreting the picture.

• Rather than using a selection of 2-D shapes, provide the children with Lego, 3-D shapes or interlocking cubes.

Page 3

Looking for Patterns

- Children need a copy of Resource sheet 17: Four square shapes, and Resource sheet 19: 2 cm squared paper for this activity.

- You may wish to tell the children to use a ruler to draw the line(s) or coloured pencils to show what shapes from the Resource sheet have been used to make each shape in the Issue, e.g.

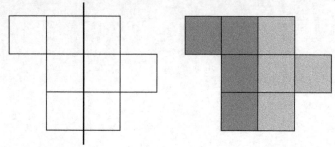

- Tell the children how many square shapes from the Resource sheet have been used to make each compound shape in the Issue, i.e.
  Shape 1: 2 square shapes
  Shape 2: 2 square shapes
  Shape 3: 3 square shapes
  Shape 4: 3 square shapes
  Shape 5: 4 square shapes
  Shape 6: 3 square shapes

Looking for Patterns

- If children have difficulty in identifying the rule, for the first, second and last patterns, tell them that the shapes have moved (rotated).

- If appropriate, ask the children to write down the rule for each of the sequences.

Page 4

The Puzzler

- Children need a copy of Resource sheet 17: Four square shapes, and Resource sheet 19: 2 cm squared paper for this activity.

- There are two aspects to this activity. Firstly, arranging each of the five different sets of shapes from Resource sheet 17 onto the 4 × 4 grid in the Issue to form squares, and secondly, identifying which of these five shapes from the Resource sheet does not fit together to form a square. If children spend too much time trying to arrange the shape that does not fit on the grid, you may need to tell the children that this is the shape that does not fit.

AfL

- How do you know that you have counted all the triangles?
- Tell me how you started to solve this puzzle.
- What is the rule for this pattern of shapes?
- What were some good words to use to describe your picture to your friend?
- Which shapes were easy to make? Which ones were a little more difficult?
- What patterns do you notice?
- Which shape did not fit onto the grid?

Answers

Page 1

Looking for Patterns
There are 5 triangles.

The Puzzler

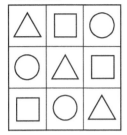

Other solutions are possible.

Page 2

Looking for Patterns

The Language of Maths
No answers required.

Page 3

Looking for Patterns

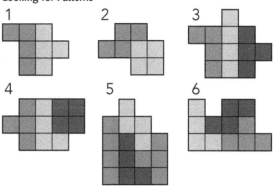

Other arrangements are possible.

Looking for Patterns

Page 4

The Puzzler

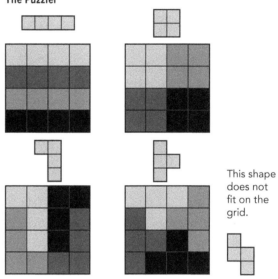

This shape does not fit on the grid.

Inquisitive ant

quadrilateral
A 2-D shape with four straight sides.

Geometry

Prerequisites for learning

- Identify patterns and relationships involving shapes
- Recognise and name common 2-D shapes and describe their features
- Use 2-D shapes to make patterns and pictures

Resources

pencil and paper

Resource sheet 2: My notes (optional)

Resource sheet 3: Pupil self assessment booklet (optional)

Resource sheet 20: Squared dot paper

sheet of coloured square paper

geoboard

elastic bands

coloured pencils

ruler

Teaching support

Page 1

Construct

- If appropriate, allow the children to work in pairs or groups to make their own origami boat. Alternatively, you may wish to work with the whole group, reading through the steps and offering assistance when and where necessary.

- Children can investigate other origami shapes.

Page 2

The Puzzler

- Ensure the children realise that each of the groups of tiles is rectangular in shape, and that the cracked lines show where each of the tiles has broken.

- Once the children have successfully completed the activity, ask them if they think that each of the sets of tiles could be even larger in size. For example, the following set of tiles could consist of 12 tiles or 14, 16, 18, 20, … tiles.

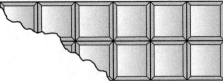

Looking for Patterns

- To assist the children in completing each of the puzzles, tell them that the six shapes climbing over the bottom grid are the missing shapes.

Page 3

The Puzzler

- You may need to spend some time discussing the puzzle with the children to ensure that they understand what they are required to do.
- Once the children have completed this activity, arrange them into pairs or a group and ask them to share their solutions. How are they different? How are they the same? Are there different correct solutions?

Construct

- If the children have already completed 🐜 The Puzzler on page 4 of Issue 33 – Geometry, then they should find this activity relatively easy.
- When the children have completed this activity, if they have also completed 🐜 The Puzzler mentioned above, then discuss with them the similarities between the two activities.

Page 4

Let's Investigate

- Encourage the children to try different shapes, for example, triangles, quadrilaterals, pentagons, hexagons and octagons.
- Once the children have completed the activity, arrange them into pairs or groups and ask them to share and discuss their shapes.

Let's Investigate

- Encourage the children to try different shaped triangles, i.e. scalene, isosceles, equilateral and right-angled triangles.
- Once the children have completed the activity, arrange them into pairs or groups and ask them to share and discuss their shapes.

AfL

- How did you work out how many tiles there were altogether in this pattern?
- How did you know that this shape belonged in this square on the puzzle?
- Is there another way that you could have divided this shape?
- Tell me about the shapes you made on the geoboard. What was the largest / smallest shape you could make that had one pin inside it? What about 2 / 3 / 4 … pins?
- Show me the shapes you drew.

Answers

Page 1

Construct
No answer required.

Page 2

The Puzzler
12 tiles   16 tiles   15 tiles

Looking for Patterns

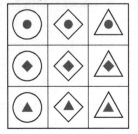   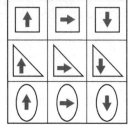

Page 3

The Puzzler

  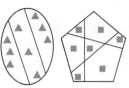

Other solutions are possible.

Construct

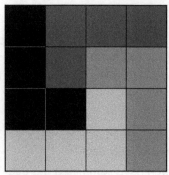

Other solutions are possible.

Page 4

Let's Investigate
Shapes will vary.

Let's Investigate
Shapes will vary.

Inquisitive ant

polygon
2-D closed shape consisting of straight sides.

Issue 35

Statistics

Prerequisites for learning

- Answer a question by recording information in lists and tables; present outcomes using practical resources or pictures
- Use diagrams to sort objects into groups according to a given criterion; suggest a different criterion for grouping the same objects

Resources

pencil and paper

Resource sheet 2: My notes (optional)

Resource sheet 3: Pupil self assessment booklet (optional)

coloured pencils

Teaching support

Page 1

Let's Investigate

- It is recommended that children complete the Inquisitive ant task (tallying) before starting on this activity.
- You may wish the children to work in pairs or groups on the second part of this activity, where they have to find out about how many people there are in the families of all the children in the class.
- Once the children have completed the activity, ensure that they have an opportunity to discuss the results and what they mean.

Page 2

The Language of Maths

- It is more than likely that there will be insufficient space in the table in the Issue for the children to write down the first names of all the children in the class. Either provide them with a larger table or limit the number of children asked to a number appropriate for the size of the class.
- When the children have completed their table, ask them to represent their results in a frequency table, i.e.

Number of letters in first name	Number of children
2	
3	
4	
5	
6	
7	
8	
more than 8	

Focus on Science

- Ensure children realise that they can group the animals into more than two groups.
- When the children have completed this activity, arrange them into pairs or groups to compare and discuss their results.

Page 3

At Home

- Once the children have completed the activity, ensure that there is an opportunity in class for pairs or groups of children to share and discuss their results.

Page 4

Focus on Science

- Children need to have completed this activity before starting on  The Language of Maths activity that follows.

- This activity needs to be introduced and started on a Monday morning, preferably during a week that is forecast to have a variety of weather.

- Ensure that there is an opportunity twice a day during the week for the children to complete their table.

- Children will need to take their copy of the Issue home at the end of the school week to complete the table.

The Language of Maths

- Children need to have completed the previous Focus on Science activity before starting on this activity.

- You may wish some children to do this activity in pairs or to complete the activity verbally rather than by writing sentences.

- When the children have completed this activity, provide an opportunity for them to compare and discuss their sentences.

AfL

- What can you tell me about these results?
- Tell me something about the information you have in this table.
- Looking at this table what do you notice?
- Ask me a question about the information in the table.

Answers

Page 1

Let's Investigate
Results of the investigation will vary.

Page 2

The Language of Maths
Results of the investigation will vary.

Focus on Science
Groupings will vary.

Page 3

At Home
Results of the investigation will vary.

Page 4

Focus on Science
Results of the investigation will vary.

The Language of Maths
Statements will vary. However, they should reflect the data from the table in the previous activity (Focus on Science).

Inquisitive ant

tallying
A simple way of counting, making a mark for each object counted, with every fifth mark used to make a group of five, i.e. ||||

Statistics

Prerequisites for learning

- Answer a question by recording information in lists and tables; present outcomes using practical resources or pictures
- Use diagrams to sort objects into groups according to a given criterion; suggest a different criterion for grouping the same objects

Resources

pencil and paper

Resource sheet 2: My notes (optional)

Resource sheet 3: Pupil self assessment booklet (optional)

1–6 dice

coloured pencils

Teaching support

Page 1

Let's Investigate

- This activity is designed to informally introduce children to the concept of chance and likelihood.
- Before setting the children to work independently on this activity, ensure that they understand what they are required to do.
- Ensure children are familiar with tally marks, i.e. ||||.
- When pairs of children have completed the activity, provide an opportunity for them to discuss their results and reasoning.

Page 2

Focus on Science

- Ensure children know what winking is. Also ensure that they ask enough children so that they make sure that their conclusions are valid.
- Before children present their results, you may like to discuss with them some of the different forms of data representation, e.g. table, frequency table, pictogram and block graph.
- Once children have presented their results, ensure that there is an opportunity for pairs of children to compare and discuss their results.

Let's Investigate

- Ensure children are familiar with tally marks, i.e. ||||.
- Some children may need assistance with writing their five most popular meals.

Page 3

Focus on Science

- Remind the children of the last question of this activity, i.e. Which objects belong in more than one column? Discuss with them how they might show this in the table.

- If appropriate, tell the children to draw, rather than write, the objects in the table. You may, however, need to provide the children with a large table in which to record their results.

Page 4

The Language of Maths

- Ensure that the children organise their list of objects in at least two different ways.

- If there are several children doing this activity, and there are two or more children with the same initial, place these children in a pair or group.

- When the children have completed the activity, arrange them into pairs or groups to compare and discuss their lists, focusing on the criteria used to sort their objects.

- A variation of this activity is to give the children a specific letter. Try and make it one that has some meaning for the class, perhaps, if appropriate, the class number / name, e.g. 1C. Children make and sort a list of all the things in the classroom, and that they can see outside, that begin with that letter.

At Home

- Once the children have completed the investigation, ensure that there is an opportunity in class for pairs or groups of children to share and discuss their results.

AfL

- Why does this object belong in more than one column in this table?
- What can you tell me about these results?
- Tell me something about the information you have in this table.
- Looking at this table what do you notice?
- What did you find out?
- Ask me a question about the information in the table.
- How did you sort your list? How else could you sort it? Are there any other ways you could organise this list?

Answers

Page 1

Let's Investigate
Explanations will vary. However, children should comment on the fact that irrespective of the number they choose the likelihood is the same.

Page 2

Focus on Science
Results of the investigation will vary.

Let's Investigate
Results of the investigation will vary.

Page 3

Focus on Science
Tables will vary.

Page 4

The Language of Maths
Lists will vary.

At Home
Lists will vary.

Inquisitive ant  graph
A special kind of chart or diagram that shows information.

Stretch and Challenge 1 Record of completion

Class/Teacher: _____

Domain(s)	Topic	Stretch and Challenge Issue	Names								
Number: – Number and place value	Number	1									
	Number	2									
	Number	3									
	Number	4									
Number: – Addition and subtraction	Addition	5									
	Addition	6									
	Subtraction	7									
	Subtraction	8									
Number: – Multiplication and division	Multiplication	9									
	Multiplication	10									
	Division	11									
	Division	12									
Number: – Addition and subtraction – Multiplication and division	Mixed operations	13									
	Mixed operations	14									
	Mixed operations	15									
	Mixed operations	16									
	Mixed operations	17									
	Mixed operations	18									

			Names									
Domain(s)	**Topic**	***Stretch and Challenge Issue***										
Number: – Fractions	Fractions	19										
	Fractions	20										
	Fractions	21										
Measurement	Length and height	22										
	Weight and mass	23										
	Capacity and volume	24										
	Time	25										
	Measurement	26										
	Measurement	27										
Geometry: – Properties of shapes	2-D shapes	28										
	3-D shapes	29										
	Patterns	30										
Geometry: – Position and direction	Position and direction	31										
	Movement	32										
Geometry: – Properties of shapes – Position and direction	Geometry	33										
	Geometry	34										
Statistics	Statistics	35										
	Statistics	36										

The Maths Herald

S&C Volume 1

Name:

Date:

I started this work on: _____

I finished this work on: _____

Inquisitive ant

The Maths Herald

s&C Volume 1

Name:

Date:

I started this work on:

I finished this work on:

This is what I learnt

I used these things to help me

I'd also like to say…

My teacher's comments

This is what I enjoyed the most

This is what I didn't enjoy

The work was:

too easy

just about right

too hard

What I could do next

1–20 number cards (1)

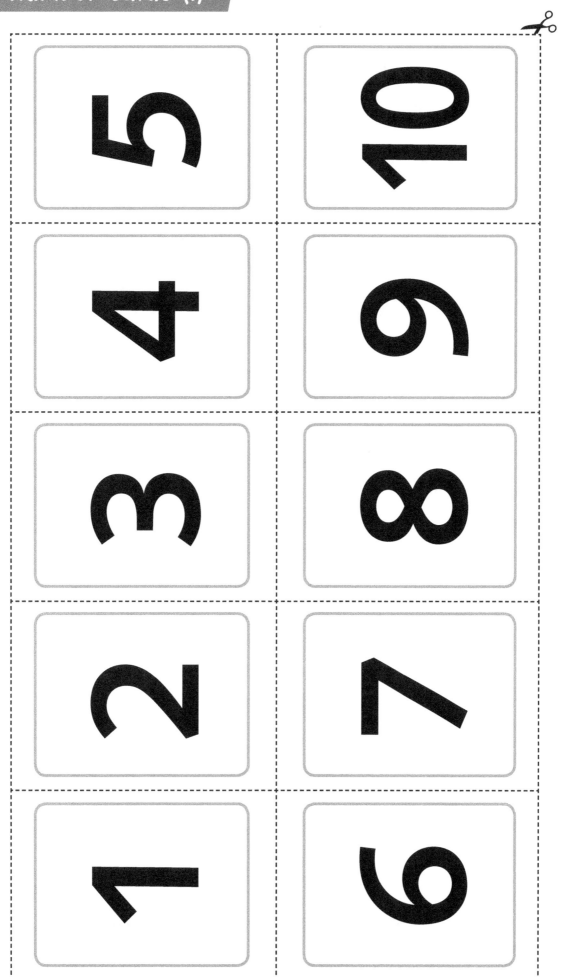

1–20 number cards (2)

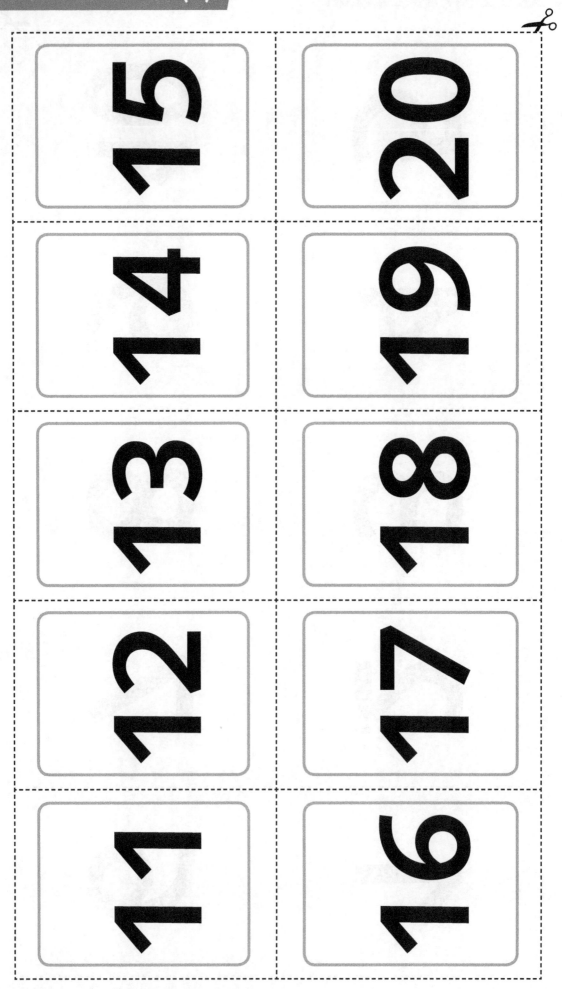

1–9 grid puzzle

Use the clues to write the digits 1 to 9 in the grid.

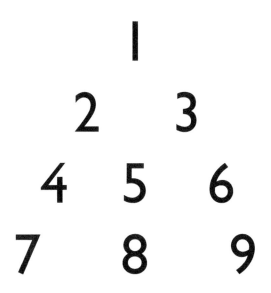

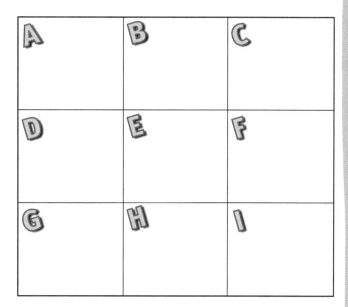

A _____

B _____

C _____

D _____

E _____

F _____

G _____

H _____

I _____

Dogs, cats and chickens

Balance
this scale
with
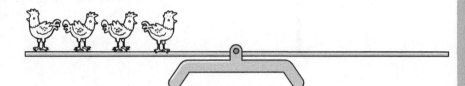

Balance
this scale
with

Balance
this scale
with

Balance
this scale
with

Bookshelf

Halves

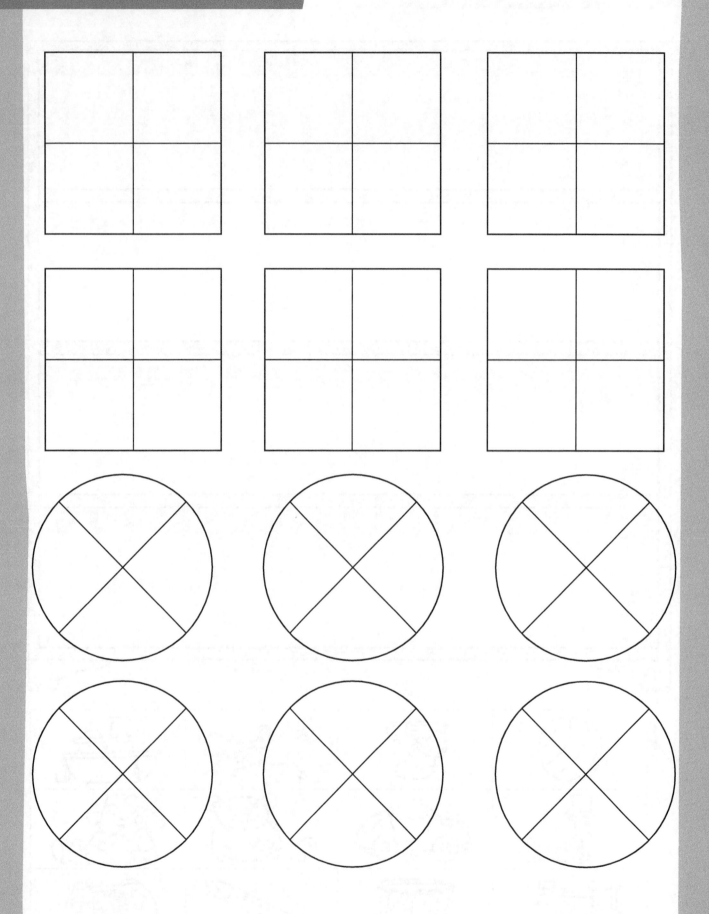

Quarters

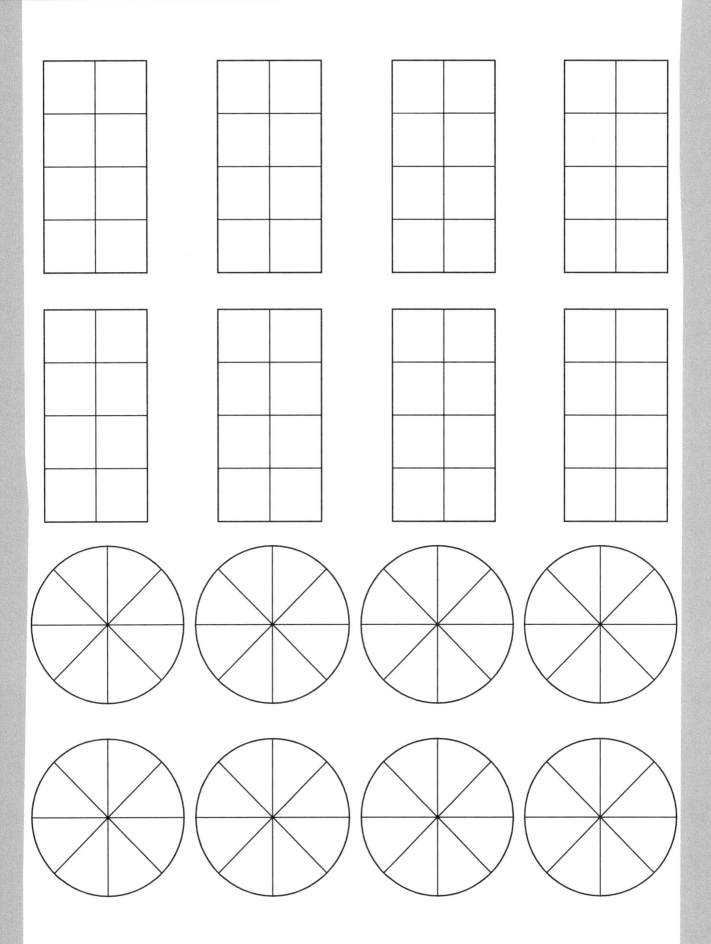

Times of the day

_____ 's day

_____ 's day

_____ 's day

Greek cross puzzles

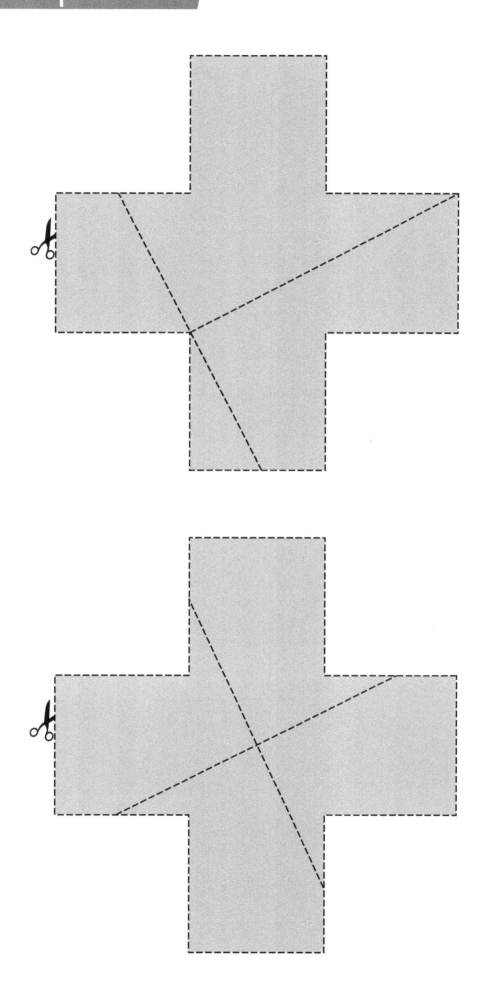

2-D shapes

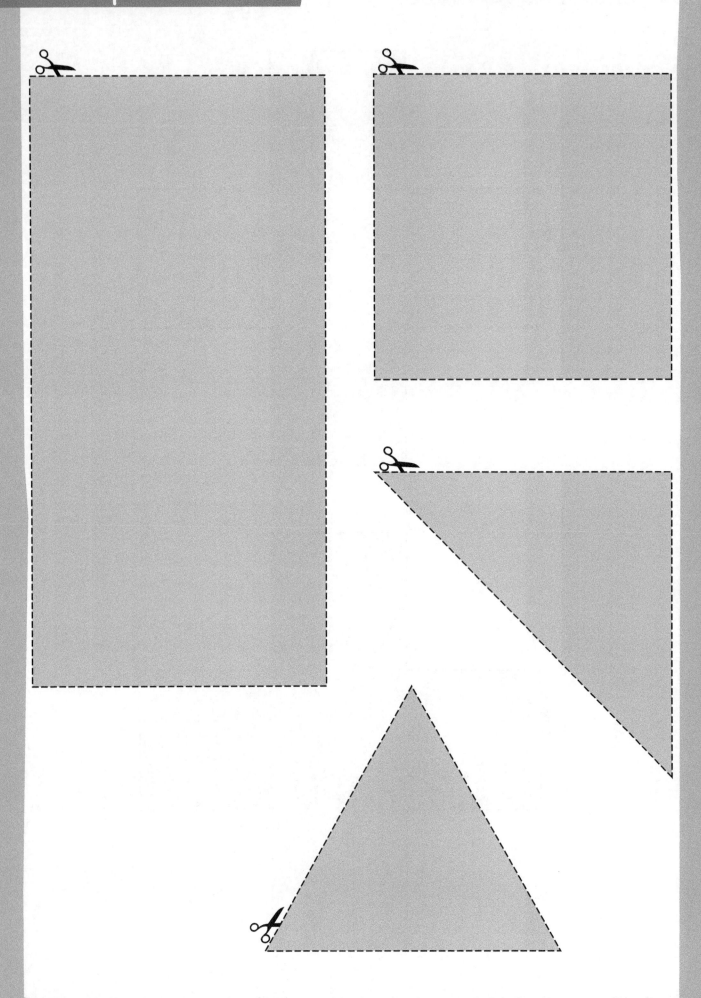

Triangle shapes

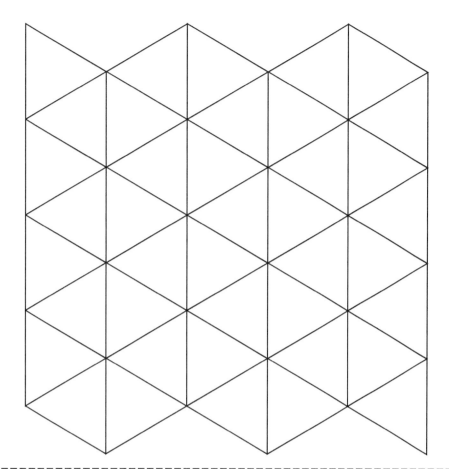

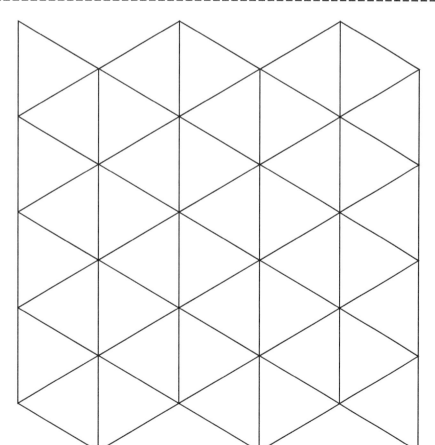

House

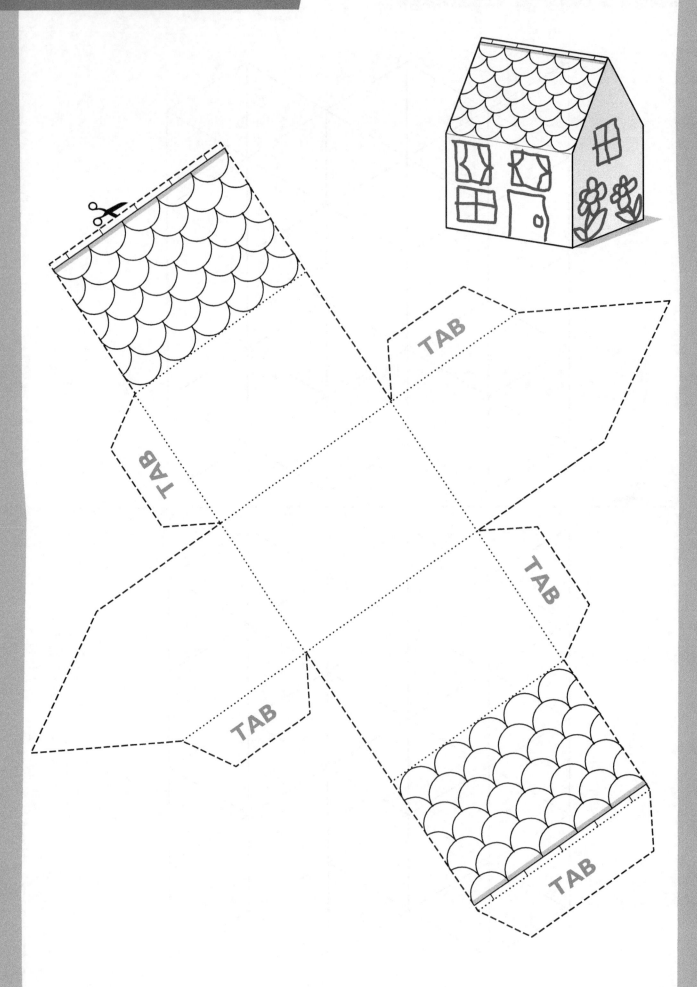

Symmetrical patterns

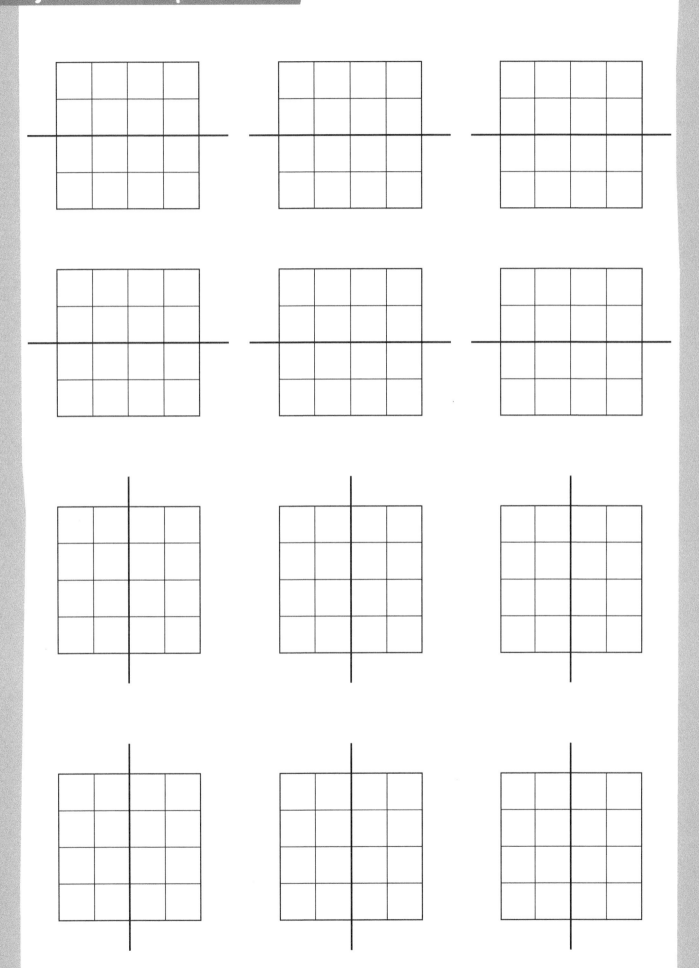

Symmetrical game

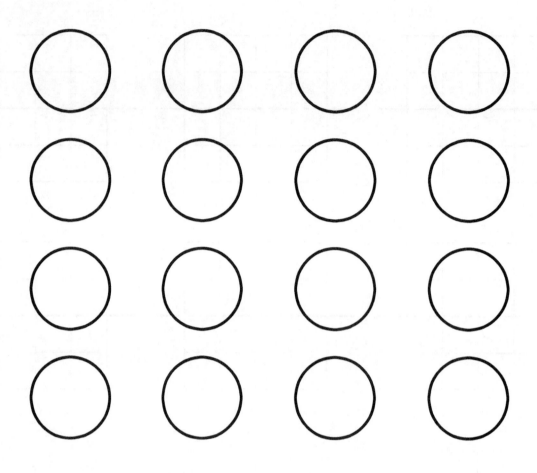

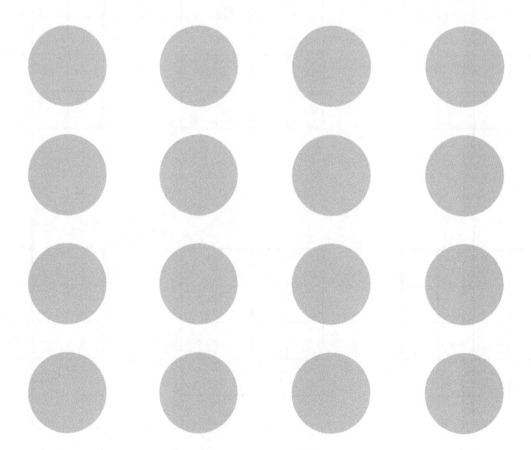

Four square shapes

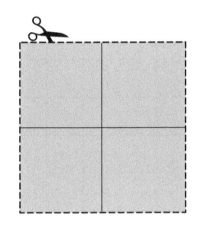

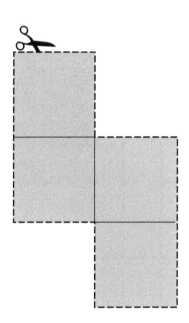

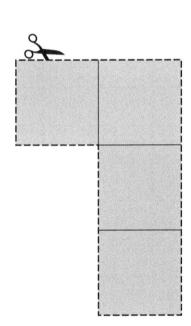

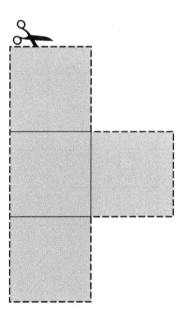

1 cm squared paper

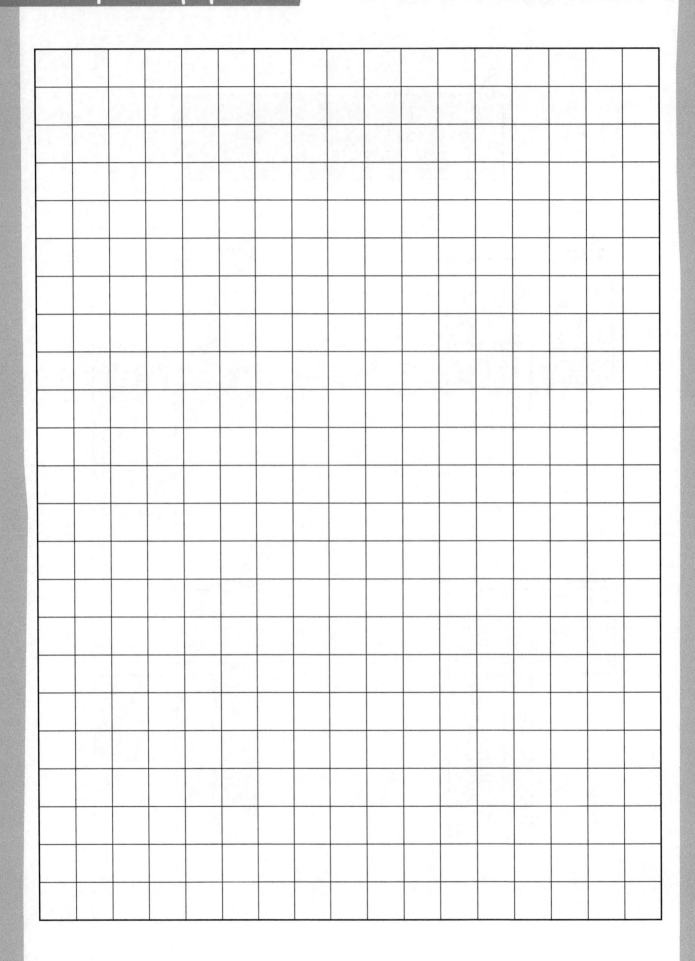

2 cm squared paper

Squared dot paper